LIFE AS A SLAVE

SLAVERY AND SLAVE RESISTANCE

LIFE AS A SLAVE

RICHARD WORTH

Enslow Publishing
101 W. 23rd Street
Suite 240
New York, NY 10011
USA

enslow.com

Published in 2017 by Enslow Publishing, LLC
101 W. 23rd Street, Suite 240, New York, NY 10011

Library of Congress Cataloging-in-Publication Data

Names: Worth, Richard, author.
Title: Life as a slave / Richard Worth.
Description: New York, NY : Enslow Publishing, 2017 | Series: Slavery and slave resistance | Includes bibliographical references and index.
Identifiers: LCCN 2015044857 | ISBN 9780766075498 (library bound)
Subjects: LCSH: Plantation life—Southern States—History—Juvenile literature. | Slaves—Southern States—Social conditions—Juvenile literature. | Slavery—Southern States—History—Juvenile literature. | Southern States—Social conditions—Juvenile literature. | Southern States—Race relations—Juvenile literature.
Classification: LCC E443 .W668 2016 | DDC 306.3/620975--dc23
LC record available at http://lccn.loc.gov/2015044857

Printed in the United States of America

To Our Readers: We have done our best to make sure all website addresses in this book were active and appropriate when we went to press. However, the author and the publisher have no control over and assume no liability for the material available on those websites or on any websites they may link to. Any comments or suggestions can be sent by e-mail to customerservice@enslow.com.

Portions of this book originally appeared in the book *Slave Life on the Plantation: Prisons Beneath the Sun.*

CONTENTS

CHAPTER 1

SLAVERY AMID FREEDOM

In 1783, when America finally won its freedom from Great Britain, every state in the union embraced slavery. Virginia had the most slaves, many of whom tilled the tobacco fields. Thomas Jefferson, author of the Declaration of Independence which declared that "All men are created equal," had numerous slaves on his plantation. George Washington, who had led the Continental Army to victory over the British, was also a slave owner.

William Grimes was born in 1784, a year later on a large and very prosperous plantation in Virginia. His father was the white plantation owner; his mother was a black slave. It was not uncommon among white masters and their female slaves to have children together. When he was only ten years old, Grimes was

THE PARTING "Buy us too."

Slavery was a centuries-old institution that destroyed lives and ripped families apart. It has left scars so deep that repercussions continue to affect American society today.

sold to another master in Virginia. At first, he was well-treated and put to work inside the main house. However, according to Grimes, other slaves who worked hard in the fields became jealous of his position. One morning, after he made coffee for the master and his family, another slave slipped medicine into it. This gave the coffee a bad taste. Grimes was given fifty lashes with a whip for what the master thought he had done.

Shortly afterward, Grimes was ordered to hoe corn in the fields. After Grimes's job was done, the master requested that he be returned to work inside the house. But Grimes refused, fearing that he might get into more trouble. Instead, he continued to work outside, under the direction of an African-American overseer, or field boss. Year later, grimes wrote about his experience: "After working with him some time, he set us to making fence, and would compel us to run with the rails on our backs, whipping us all the time most unmercifully. This hard treatment continuing for some time I at length resolved to run away."[1]

Grimes escaped, but he was caught and whipped. This did not prevent him from escaping again. But again he was captured, and the whippings continued. How did slaves like Grimes endure this treatment? As he put it: "If it were not for our hopes, our hearts would

Run away from the subscriber in Albermarle, a Mulatto slave called Sandy, about 35 years of age, his stature is rather low, inclining to corpulence, and his complexion light; he is a shoemaker by trade, in which he uses his left hand principally, can do coarse carpenters work, and is something of a horse jockey... Whoever conveys the said slave to me...shall have 40 s. (shilling) reward....[2]
—Thomas Jefferson, in a 1769 newspaper advertisement to capture one of his runaway slaves.

break; we poor slaves always cherish hopes of better times."[3] Eventually, Grimes was given to his master's son, a doctor, and taken to another part of Virginia, where he received treatment that was not as cruel. Along the way, he was reunited with his mother and brothers. He had been separated from them years earlier when they were sold. It was quite common in the South for a master to split up slave families— keep some and sell others when he needed to raise money.

Grimes was eventually sold by the doctor. In all, he would have ten different masters. Some were very cruel. Grimes even tried to break his own leg and later starve himself, so he might be sold to someone who treated him better.

Finally, in about 1814, another escape opportunity arose while he was living with a new master in Savannah, Georgia. He was loading bales of cotton onto a ship that had come from Boston. The sailors, who were northerners, befriended Grimes. They arranged for him to sail with them when they left Savannah. As he said, "they proposed to me to leave in the center of the cotton bales on deck, a hole or place sufficiently large for me to stow away in, with my necessary provisions."[4] With their help, Grimes reached the North and freedom. He published an account of his life in 1824.

Grimes's story of harsh treatment at the hands of his masters is not unusual. Delia Garlic, another slave, worked on plantations for thirty years in three states. Once, her mistress—the woman who owned her—became so angry with Delia that she struck her with a piece of firewood and knocked her out. Delia was sold away from her mother and sent to Louisiana.

William and Ellen Craft were also slaves in the South. Ellen's mother was a slave, but her father was a white planter. In fact, she was so light-skinned that she almost looked white. Ellen's husband William was a cabinetmaker. His master had decided that William should learn a trade so he could be hired out to other plantations. This practice was quite common in the South. It was a way for masters to earn extra money from the work of their slaves.

As William explained, his master

had the reputation of being a very humane and Christian man, but he thought nothing of selling my poor old father, and dear aged mother, at separate times, to different persons, to be dragged off never to behold each other again. . . . The reason he assigned for disposing of my parents, as well as of several other aged slaves, was, that "they were getting old, and would soon become valueless in the market, and therefore he intended to sell off all the old stock, and buy in a young lot."[5]

William Craft's master ran into financial problems. He needed money and auctioned William, along with his sister. His sister was sold first, and then it was William's turn to be auctioned.

I saw the cart in which she sat moving slowly off; and, as she clasped her hands with a grasp that indicated despair, and looked pitifully round towards me, I also saw the large silent tears trickling down her cheeks. She made a farewell bow, and buried her face in her lap.[6]

The separation and sale of slave families was repeated thousands of times throughout the slaveholding states. William Craft feared that the same thing would happen again after he met and married Ellen. Slave owners did not recognize slave marriages. A married couple could be separated and sold at any time. As a result, William and Ellen Craft decided on a daring escape plan to preserve their relationship. During the 1840s, they left the South and reached freedom in Philadelphia.

The stories of William Grimes, Delia Garlic, and William and Ellen Craft are typical of the lives endured by thousands and thousands of African Americans as slaves on southern plantations.

CHAPTER 2

THE BEGINNINGS OF SLAVERY

John Rolfe is probably best known as the husband of the Native American princess Pochahontas. But he also served as governor of Virginia. Perhaps even more important for the colony, he introduced the widespread growing of tobacco. This was a cash crop, sold in Europe, that helped to make the fortunes of many Virginia planters. To sow and harvest the crop, the planters relied on African Americans, who began to arrive in Virginia in 1619. The first arrivals, brought by a Dutch slave trader, were purchased by Rolfe. Whether they were slaves or servants, historians are uncertain.[1]

What is certain, however, is that these were not the first Africans to be shipped to the New World. For more than a century, African slaves had worked in the Caribbean and South America. They tilled the soil and worked in the mines of the Spanish and Portuguese colonies. In 1492, the Spanish king and queen, Ferdinand and Isabella, sent Christopher Columbus on a historic voyage of exploration. Columbus was convinced that he could find a route to the Spice Islands of Asia by sailing west. Instead, he encountered the islands of the Caribbean Sea in the New World.

On the island of Hispaniola in the Caribbean Sea, Columbus started a Spanish colony. There, he met a tribe of peaceful Caribbean Indians known as the Taíno. Columbus enslaved the Taínos. He wanted them to work the gold mines on the island as well as the fields of large Spanish estates on Hispaniola.

Soon, the Taíno caught European diseases, such as measles and smallpox. These diseases had been brought by the Spanish from Europe. The Taínos had never been exposed to these diseases and had no immunity to them. They died by the thousands and were almost wiped out.

As a result, the Spanish had to turn to a new source of slaves. Since the middle of the fifteenth century, Portuguese merchants had been trading in slaves from the coast of West Africa. It was a profitable business. The Portuguese established trading posts along the coastline. They sold European goods, such as bracelets, knives, and swords, to the African tribal leaders. In return, the Portuguese received black slaves. Some of these slaves were taken to Portugal and Spain to work on sugar plantations. Others worked on flourishing plantations on the islands of São Tomé and Príncipe. These islands are located in the Gulf of Guinea in western Africa.

By the early sixteenth century, the Portuguese were taking some of these slaves to the New World. There, they worked on the sugar plantations in the Spanish colonies. They also worked in the colony of Brazil, established by the Portuguese themselves. In addition, African slaves were forced to work in the huge Spanish silver mine of Potosí in Peru. Between 1525 and 1575, an estimated 73,500 African slaves were sent to the Spanish and Portuguese colonies. This number would double to about 150,000 during the first quarter of the seventeenth century.[2]

THE EARLY YEARS OF SLAVERY IN NORTH AMERICA

By the early seventeenth century, the Dutch had also entered the slave trading business. Dutch ship captains brought most of the slaves to the Caribbean and South America. But some were also shipped to the Dutch colony of New Amsterdam (later called New York). Others were brought to English colonies in the South, like Virginia.

At first, however, there was a very small demand for slaves. Instead, the English colonists relied on another source of workers: indentured servants. These were people who signed on to work for a specific period of time, usually four or five years. In return, they were given free passage to the New World. Some of the indentured servants came to the colonies to escape prison for find work. After their indenture was complete, they could obtain land.

Indenture had existed in Europe for centuries. Therefore, the colonists thought nothing of hiring indentured servants to work their land in the New World. Many of these servants came to the colonies of Virginia and Maryland. Here, they worked on plantations that grew tobacco and corn.

During the first half of the seventeenth century, there was a steady supply of indentured servants. They often worked side by side with the plantation owners. In addition, the plantations had a small number of captured American Indians and Africans. While some of the Africans may have been slaves, others were indentured servants. As one white indentured servant put it: "We and the Negroes both alike did fare/Of work and food we had an equal share. . . ."[3] Even the enslaved could become free. In some cases, the Africans were freed by the will of a plantation owner, following his death. These Africans

Fabbricazione del Tabacco

Slaves were brought to the American colonies to provide free labor for tobacco plantations and other endeavors. Early on, slaves were afforded some rights, but restrictive laws were soon enacted.

Bennardoni inc:

received land and began to establish their own tobacco plantations.

Anthony Johnson, for example, had been brought to Jamestown in 1621. He was sold to the Bennett family and worked on their tobacco plantation. While he was owned by the Bennetts, Johnson was permitted to have his own small farm and get married. Eventually, Johnson and his family were given their freedom. They established their own plantation on the eastern shore of Virginia.[4]

During this period, there were few laws governing slaves because there were very few of them. In 1650, Virginia had only three hundred African slaves out of a total settler population of fifteen thousand. In Maryland, there was the same number of slaves out of a population of over four thousand.[5] While they worked on the plantations, slaves had time to farm for themselves. They were also permitted to own animals, such as pigs and chickens. This enabled them to add to the small amount of food received from the plantation owners. The slaves also grew corn and tobacco, which they were permitted to sell. Some became expert carpenters and shoemakers. They sometimes received tips for exceptional work. With the money they earned by selling crops or skills, some slaves eventually purchased their freedom.

SLAVERY GROWS AND CHANGES

During the last half of the seventeenth century, events occurred in England that changed the nature of slavery in North America. The number of indentured servants began to decline. In 1660, a new king, Charles II, brought stability back to England following years of civil war. As a result, the economy began to improve and more jobs were available. Therefore, the demand for workers—as well as their pay—increased. The opportunities in the English colonies seemed less attractive. Indentured servants had hoped for land after their indenture was over. However, plantation owners were reluctant to provide any land to newly freed indentured servants. The planters regarded the former servants as competitors.[6]

Gradually, the supply of indentured servants declined. Although a few American Indians worked on the plantations, they did not satisfy the plantation owners. Male American Indians had been raised to believe that farming was work that should be done by women. Therefore, they were unreliable workers. They could also escape easily, hide in the forests—which they knew well, and return to their tribes.

To deal with this problem, the colonists began to import more and more African slaves. In Virginia and Maryland, the number of Africans more than tripled, reaching about 4,600 between 1660 and 1680. Slaves were primarily brought from the West Indies in the Caribbean.[7] Many of these slaves already had experience working on plantations, and they often spoke English. The cost of slaves was higher than that of indentured servants. But, unlike servants, slaves could be held for life. Because of their skin color, it was also more difficult for them to escape and blend in with the rest of the population.

Over the next half century, the number of Africans continued to increase. In Virginia, the African population grew from two thousand in 1670 to six thousand by 1700. By that same year, the slave population in Maryland had reached over three thousand from less than half that number thirty years earlier.[8]

At the same time, the slave population also increased in the northern colonies. They worked on the farms and in ports such as Philadelphia and New York. However, there were far fewer slaves in the northern colonies. Most of the farms in the north were small and produced only food crops to feed the farmers and their families. These were not cash crops, like tobacco, that were grown for export.

Tobacco plantations required a steady supply of labor that was tied to the land and could not leave it. Without workers, the plantations could not produce the crops that the owners needed to make profits. Plantation owners realized that they could make even more money if they used slaves, because they did not have to pay them.

In 1674, the British established the Royal African Company. The company was given a monopoly by the government to purchase slaves in Africa and import them to the New World. Thus, the British government encouraged slave trade to the colonies.

Over the next two decades, the company would bring ninety thousand slaves to the western hemisphere.[9] The majority of them went to the British colonies in the Caribbean, such as Jamaica and Barbados. But some slaves were also brought to North America. There, they worked on the tobacco plantations of the South. Over five hundred slaves came into Virginia in 1679, for example. Another nine hundred slaves were brought into Virginia during the middle of the next decade.[10]

By the end of the century, the British government had permitted other companies to become involved the slave trade. Competition reduced the prices of slaves. Therefore, planters could afford to buy more of them. Meanwhile, rising tobacco prices gave planters more money and made slaves even more affordable.

The growth in the slave population of the South paralleled the increase in tobacco output. In 1619, when Africans first arrived in the New World, twenty thousand pounds of tobacco were produced. By 1700, the tobacco crop had grown to thirty-eight million pounds.[11]

This is an example of a certificate of indenture. Sixteen-year-old Shadrach was indentured to landowner James Morris. His term of servitude was set to last for 11 years, 5 months, and 25 days.

Most of the tobacco plantations were small. The plantation owners worked them with only a few slaves. In Maryland, for example, most plantations had less than ten slaves. About half of the plantations had only one or two slaves.[12] In South Carolina, however, the colonists established rice plantations. These required a great deal of irrigation to supply water to the rice plants. It was more economical to develop large plantations that required far more slaves.

Black Africans, according to historian Peter Kolchin, were regarded differently from white servants. They were considered unclean because of their color and their non-Christian beliefs.[13] These factors created prejudice against them among the white colonists. According to historian Edmund Morgan, as the number of Africans began to increase after the middle of the century, the depth of this prejudice increased, too. Along with it, fear of a slave revolt began to rise among the white population.[14]

NEW LAWS CONTROL THE LIVES OF SLAVES

To control the increasing population of slaves, colonies began to pass a series of laws to restrict them. In 1668, for example, the Virginia legislature, known as the House of Burgesses, passed a law that allowed a master to use any kind of punishment he wanted on a slave. Some masters were already known to whip a slave repeatedly if he or she ran away or disobeyed.

In 1676, a civil war known as Bacon's Rebellion broke out in Virginia. It was led by Nathaniel Bacon, a member of the Virginia legislature. Bacon disagreed with the policies of the colonial governor, Sir William Berkeley, and the planters who supported him. The rebellion was joined by some slaves and indentured servants who wanted to gain their freedom. Although Bacon was at first successful, he died in the fall of 1676. The rebellion was put down by Berkeley's troops.

Following the rebellion, Virginians were fearful of future alliances between slaves and servants. The state legislature passed more severe

In time, the slave trade became a profitable global network. Greater numbers of Africans were kidnapped, packed like animals onto ships, and brought to North America.

laws to control slaves. They were prohibited from carrying weapons. They were required to have passes to travel off the plantation. If they tried to escape and were caught by their owner, they could be killed. In 1691, marriage was prohibited between a white person and a black

The colony of Virginia's government passed this slave code in 1705. They believed this law would help prevent slave rebellions by not letting the slaves carry guns. At the time, the English language was not as standardized as it is now. As a result, many of the words in the below text are misspelled by today's standards.

WHEREAS the frequent meeting of considerable numbers of negroe slaves under pretence of feasts and buriells is judged of dangerous consequence . . . it shall not be lawfull for any negroe or other slave to carry or arme himselfe with any club, staffe, gunn, sword or any other weapon of defence or offence, nor to goe or depart from of his masters ground without a certificate from his master, mistris or overseer, and such permission not to be granted but upon perticuler and necessary occasions; and every negroe or slave soe offending not haveing a certificate as aforesaid shalbe sent to the next constable, who is hereby enjoyned and required to give the said negroe twenty lashes on his bare back well layd on, and soe sent home to his said master, mistris or overseer. . . . if any negroe or other slave shall presume to lift up his hand in opposition against any christian, shall for every such offence, upon due proofe made thereof by the oath of the party before a magistrate, have and receive thirty lashes on his bare back well laid on. . . .[15]

person. A year later, the legislature ordered that plantation owners take "'all cattle [and] hoggs . . . by any slave kept.'"[16]

Meanwhile, similar laws were being passed in Maryland. In 1664, the colonial legislature ordered that all slaves should remain in bondage for their entire lives. A law in 1695 required that slaves carry passes to travel away from their plantations. While slaves were permitted to marry each other, they were prohibited from marrying white people. In Maryland, however, masters were not allowed to mistreat their slaves. They were expected to provide them with food, a place to live, and clothes to wear. Nevertheless, one slave owner who killed his slave for misbehavior and running away was found not guilty of any crime.[17]

In South Carolina, the slave laws were equally harsh. Many of the settlers of this colony had come from the British island of Barbados. In Barbados, there were large sugar plantations worked by slaves. Planters who left Barbados often brought their slaves with them. They wanted laws that would be similar to those on Barbados. In 1696, a law stated that strict controls of Africans were necessary because of their "'barbarous, wild, savage Natures' and because they were 'naturally prone and inclined' to 'Disorders . . . and Inhumanity.'"[18]

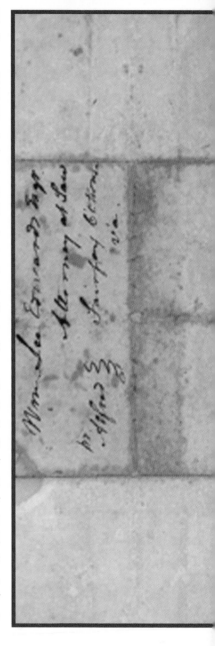

This pass, issued to a slave named Alfred, was proof of license to travel in and around Washington, DC. Traveling without official permission could result in punishment.

By the end of the seventeenth century, southern colonies had passed a series of laws to ensure that Africans always remained slaves. There were a few exceptions. Historian Whittington B. Johnson wrote that if a slave could show that he had an agreement with his master to work for only a specific length of time, then he could be freed.[19] But these were very rare exceptions; most enslaved Africans remained slaves for life.

CHAPTER 3

SLAVERY IN THE 18TH CENTURY

They came across the Atlantic Ocean—known as the Middle Passage—by the thousands. The slaves were packed into the holds of ships on the west African coast, then transported to America on a journey that took anywhere from five weeks to three months. Although some of the slaves died because of the harsh conditions aboard ship, many were eventually landed in the American colonies.

Historians estimate that approximately ten thousand slaves came to Virginia during the first twenty years of the eighteenth century. Over the next three decades, another thirty thousand arrived on the slave ships.[1] By 1750, over two hundred thousand slaves lived in the colonies.[2] Approximately forty percent of the population of Virginia was enslaved.

Ex-slave Moses Grandy described the difficulty of working in a rice bog:

I have said this M'Pherson was an overseer where slaves were employed in cutting canals. The labour there is very severe. The ground is often very boggy: the negroes are up to the middle or much deeper in mud and water, cutting away roots and baling out mud: if they can keep their heads above water, they work on.[3]

The majority of the residents in South Carolina were Africans.[4] Many were brought in British ships, but others came on colonial vessels.

Merchants from Newport, Rhode Island, for example, began a vast triangular trade. They traded rum to the people of Africa in return for slaves. Some slaves were brought to the plantations of the West Indies and traded for molasses and sugar. These goods were transported to Rhode Island and made into rum. Newport merchants also brought slaves directly to the South and sold them to the plantation owners.

Many slaves were also brought to Charleston, South Carolina. They were sold to the rice planters in the Carolinas and Georgia. Some planters hurried onto the slave ships in the harbor. They purchased slaves directly from the sea captains. This was a procedure known as scrambling. Other planters purchased their slaves at auction. By 1750, an estimated forty thousand slaves lived in South Carolina and Georgia. Even in northern states, there were over thirty thousand slaves.[5]

Each rice plantation employed a large number of slaves—at least fifty and often over one hundred workers. "Sowing began in April and sometimes lasted into June," wrote historian Ira Berlin,

with barefoot slaves pressing the seeds into waterlogged muck with their heels. . . . Slaves then flooded the fields to encourage germination. Once the seeds sprouted, the fields had to be hoed to suppress the weeds . . . for a large portion of the year, slaves labored knee-deep in stagnant muck, surrounded by buzzing insects, under the scorching sun.

The water was then removed from the fields, but "the insects remained, and they were joined by a host of slithering reptiles. . . ." In the fall, the rice was finally harvested, but soon afterward the slaves returned to the fields to prepare them for another crop.[6]

On the plantations, the slaves operated under the task system. They were expected to complete a certain number of tasks each day.

Plantation slaves lived in crude cabins on the master's property. While slaves were often allowed to marry, have families, and live in their own quarters, they could just as easily be separated forever.

Once these had been finished, the slaves were free to pursue their own activities. To help feed themselves, they developed their own gardens, growing corn, potatoes, peanuts, and other crops.

That amount of free time made it easier for slaves to create their own distinctive culture. The majority of slaves brought from Africa came from areas located in present day Nigeria or Angola. After they were sold at auction, the slaves were transported together to a plantation. Along the way, they developed some bonds of friendship. Once they reached the plantation and went to work in the fields, these bonds often strengthened. The majority of slaves brought from Africa were men, but there were also some women. Slaves married and produced children. However, in the eyes of the laws passed by the colonial legislatures, slaves were not considered legally married.

SLAVE LIFE ON THE PLANTATIONS

Northward on the tobacco plantations of Maryland and Virginia, slave families also were being formed. As historian Allan Kulikoff has pointed out, many female slaves suffered on the long trip that brought them from Africa. The harsh conditions on the slave ships and the lack of food undermined the health of the female slaves. This meant that they could often bear few children after they reached North America. By the middle of the century, however, many children had reached adulthood on the plantations. They began to form their own families. These women married as teenagers and gave birth to six to eight children.[7]

Slaves resisted their unfair lot by reacting in different ways. Some lashed out physically, while others attempted escape. If caught, a fugitive slave was subject to harsh punishment.

Historians believe that an abundance of food helped these families to thrive. In addition, working in the tobacco fields was not as harsh on women as the work on the sugar plantations was in the Caribbean islands. Far fewer children were born there.

Slave families lived in cabins, known as the slave quarters. In some cases, married couples were fortunate enough to be together on the same plantation. Indeed, Robert Carter, a rich Virginia planter with several plantations, encouraged his slaves to marry. As historian Lorena Walsh has pointed out, married slaves "were much less likely to try to run away than were unattached individuals. . . . Whenever possible, Carter kept husbands and wives together on the same plantation and allotted them a house to themselves."[8]

Running away was a common way in which slaves resisted their masters. Some male slaves left plantations and hid out for a year or two in the woods. Because many plantations were small, however, a male and a female slave from neighboring plantations might form a family. Plantation owners permitted slaves to visit each other.

Gradually, slaves began to form large family networks. Sometimes, parents, grandparents, aunts, and uncles lived on the same plantation. Children grew up surrounded by many relatives. They might be cared for by an aunt or a grandmother. But a white master might sell a family member to a neighboring plantation. Then a slave family had to work much harder to maintain its connections. This might involve visits between plantations.

A DISTINCT CULTURE

Slaves developed a culture that was a mixture of African and American influences. Their language, for example, often included English as well as African words. The slaves' religion also reflected a combination of African as well as Christian beliefs, adopted from colonial society. From Africa, the slaves brought a strong belief that spirits inhabited nature. They believed that spirits could be found in trees, in rocks, in the sky, and in the land. The slaves relied on magicians and witch doctors to banish evil spirits and encourage the work of good spirits. To protect their homes, slaves put shiny metal and glass in trees to ward off evil spirits.

Once loved ones had died, slaves believed that their spirits would return to the places where they had lived. As slaves embraced Christianity, however, this belief was gradually replaced with one that placed the dead spirits in heaven.[9]

During the 1740s and 1750s, North America was gripped by a religious revival called the Great Awakening. Among its leaders was George Whitefield, a Methodist minister from England. He preached to white congregations and called on them to treat their slaves more humanely. Whitefield also visited with many slaves and brought the message of Christianity to them. The message of Christianity—that everyone was equal in the sight of God—seemed to kindle a hope among many slaves that they might eventually be freed. Some southerners who participated in the Great Awakening may have also begun to realize that slavery was an injustice.[10] However, slave owners did not begin to free their slaves as a result of the Great Awakening. Nor did many slaves embrace Christianity, according to historians Marvin Kay and Lorin Cary. They wrote that "only a small percentage had been successfully proselytized [converted to Christianity]."[11]

Another area that reflected African and American influences was the naming of slaves. Frequently, these names were given to slaves by their white owners in the South and the North. Common names were Jack and Will for men and Betty or Kate for women. Some slaves were also named after places, like York or Bristol in England. They might also be given names from the ancient world, such as Caesar or Hercules. But, unknown to their white masters, the slaves also kept the names they had brought from Africa. These might be names like Tambo or Ubaka. Some slaves even named their children after deceased ancestors. This was a way of bringing back their spirits into a new generation and connecting families subject to separation.

THE WORK OF SLAVES

Many slaves who lived on plantations, both male and female, worked as field hands. They tended tobacco or rice crops. As the numbers of slaves increased, however, more and more became specialists in other areas. On George Washington's plantation in Virginia, for example, there were four carpenters, two blacksmiths, and two seamstresses.[12] Plantation owners often tried to make their estates as self-sufficient as possible. Learning these skilled occupations gave slaves a better job than the common field hands who labored in the hot sun all day.

Slaves who worked in the master's house also avoided the back-breaking labor of field hands. Slaves called their owner's home the "great house," regardless of its size. Large slave owners had magnificent homes, like Thomas Jefferson's Monticello. But many white slave owners had much smaller homes. Slaves who worked in the great house handled the cooking and cleaning. They often cared for the children of the plantation owners. Some male slaves served as valets for their masters, keeping their clothes ironed and cleaned. Female slaves carried out similar duties for their mistresses. Male slaves also worked as coachmen, driving the carriage of the master or mistress as they went into town or visited another plantation.

Slaves not only lived on the plantations, but in the cities, as well. Charleston, Savannah, and Williamsburg, for example, included many slaves. They worked for the artisans and other residents in these cities. Historian Philip Morgan wrote that among the occupations of male slaves in Charleston during the eighteenth century were carpenters, shoemakers, bricklayers, butchers, barbers, and painters.[13]

Slaves who were not continually busy with work given them by their masters were permitted to hire themselves out to other people. Some were even permitted to live apart from their owners. They were also allowed to keep part of the money they earned, and gave the rest of it to their masters. With these earnings, some slaves bought their freedom.

However, slaves who hired out were sometimes resented by white artisans. According to historian Michele Gillespie, they believed that

Domestic slaves worked in the home, cooking, cleaning, and minding the children. Often, the children of the house were raised alongside slave children.

their wages were reduced because of competition from African Americans. Sometimes the artisans might even retaliate by beating these slaves. As one slave recalled: "I was beat and tortured most cruelly, and was laid up three weeks before I was able to do any work."[14]

African Americans, however, managed to survive. On paper, the slave laws often seemed to control their entire lives. In reality, some slaves achieved at least a little independence. Some slaves worked as peddlers. They sold not only food grown by their masters but items that the slaves themselves had acquired in trade. This gave them a steady source of income, which they kept for themselves. In Charleston, slaves also made money by fishing and selling their fish on the piers.

CHANGING ATTITUDES TOWARD SLAVES

During the last half of the eighteenth century, an intellectual movement in Europe called the Enlightenment had significant impact on slaves' lives. It emphasized that human beings could be perfected and that no one should be kept back by artificial bonds. The English religious leader, George Whitefield, reflected this belief. He wrote: "Blacks

Skilled slaves were sometimes rented out to local artisans. This did not make them exempt from racist treatment, however, and their masters benefitted from their earnings.

are just as much, and no more, conceived and born in sin, as white men are; and both, if born and bred up here, I am persuaded, are naturally capable of the same improvement."[15]

The ideas of the Enlightenment together with those of the Great Awakening influenced plantation owners. These ideas persuaded some of them to begin questioning the morality of slavery. Gradually, a few plantation owners began to feel more responsible for the lives of their slaves. They wanted the slaves to be treated like other human beings.

Unfortunately, they had trouble regarding slaves as people just like whites. One slave owner wrote about bringing a young slave with him to become his manservant and separating him from his mother. He did not realize until later how much this separation had affected the slave. Unfortunately, he did not regard the slave as a human being like himself. As the man wrote:

> How finely woven, how delicately sensible must be those bonds of natural affection which equally adorn the civilized and savage. The American and African—nay the man and the brute! I declare I know not a situation in which I have been lately placed that touched me so nearly as that incident.[16]

Physical punishment of slaves also continued. Overseers still whipped slaves who did not carry out the work that was expected of them. They also developed other, more brutal forms of torture. During the 1770s, Philip Vickers Fithian from Connecticut was a tutor for the children of Robert Carter. He recalled that Carter's overseer said that whipping African Americans was a waste of time, "for they will laugh at your greatest severity." But he had come up with something far more effective:

> For sullenness, obstinacy, or laziness, he says, take a Negro, strip him, and tie him fast to a post. Then take a sharp curry comb [a metal comb used to brush horses] and curry him severely until he is well scraped; then call a boy with some dry hay and make

the boy rub him down for several minutes; and then salt him and release him. He will . . . attend to his business afterwards![17]

Fithian was outraged by the overseer's remarks and the immorality of slavery.

AMERICAN INDEPENDENCE

Many colonial leaders began to question the morality of slavery as a result of the revolution that broke out in 1775. As part of the Declaration of Independence, Thomas Jefferson wrote that "all men are created equal." Ironically, Jefferson himself was a slave owner with 187 slaves.[18] Some of the slaves heard about the Declaration of Independence. They began to take steps to achieve their own freedom.

In Virginia, the British colonial governor, Lord Dunmore, promised slaves their freedom. To achieve it, they had to join the British army to fight against the rebellious Americans. Approximately eight hundred slaves ran away from the plantations and enlisted with Dunmore before he was driven out of Virginia by American forces.[19] The South became the scene of a bloody civil war between Patriots [supporters of independence] and Loyalists [those who were loyal to Britain]. Plantation life was often disrupted as guerilla bands fought for control of territory in Georgia and the Carolinas. Some slaves took advantage of the opportunity to run away from the plantations. They joined the British troops who had occupied Charleston and Savannah.

Plantation owners tried to prevent more slaves from leaving. They moved the slaves inland away from the fighting. In addition, some slave owners tried to encourage rather than order their slaves to work. They believed that this might persuade them not to try to escape. In 1782, Virginia also passed a law making it easier for owners to free their slaves, which had been illegal in the past.

Historians estimate that approximately five thousand slaves from Virginia and Maryland left the plantations as a result of the war.[20]

Brave Colored Artilleryman.

With the promise of freedom hundreds of slaves fought on the side of the British in the Revolutionary War. To their dismay, the bold declarations that all men were created equal did not include blacks.

But far more remained. Indeed, historian Ira Berlin estimates that the number of slaves actually increased during the Revolutionary War. This was due to regular childbirth in slave families. More slaves also meant that more people could become slaveholders.[21]

In 1783, the United States signed a peace treaty with Great Britain to end the Revolutionary War. The British formally recognized the new nation as an independent country. Slavery remained an important part of the American economy.

SLAVERY AND THE US CONSTITUTION

In 1787, delegates from the thirteen states that formed the new American nation met in Philadelphia. This meeting was called the Constitutional Convention. The delegates replaced a weak form of central government with a stronger one under the Constitution. By this time, northern states had begun the process of freeing their slaves. Many northerners believed that the freedom gained in the American Revolution applied to everyone.

Indeed, there were fewer than four thousand slaves in New England and approximately forty thousand in the other northern states. In the South, however, slavery still played an important role in agriculture. The southern states had over 650,000 slaves.[22] In the Carolinas, for example, rice planters had been importing additional slaves. These replaced the slaves that had run off during the American Revolution. During the war, South Carolina had lost an estimated twenty-five thousand slaves, and Georgia had lost ten thousand.[23]

Slavery was already a divisive issue between northern and southern delegates. Some northern delegates wanted to end slavery in the United States. To build support for the Constitution, the founding fathers decided not to tackle the issue of slavery at the Constitutional Convention. They let slavery remain in the areas where it was practiced. The founders who opposed slavery feared that if they tried to end it, the southern delegates would not give their support to the Constitution. This would leave the new nation with a weak government. The delegates at the convention could only agree to eliminate the slave trade to and from Africa by 1808.

A few years after the Constitutional Convention, in the 1790s, a Connecticut schoolteacher named Eli Whitney developed the cotton gin. This enabled slaves to separate cotton fiber from its seeds much faster. Cotton plantations increased. Slavery would now become even more important to the southern economy.

CHAPTER 4

THE IMPACT OF COTTON ON SLAVERY

Throughout history, a single invention has possessed the power to transform an entire culture. In the 1400s, Johannes Guttenberg introduced the printing press, increasing the spread of books and new ideas across Europe. In the mid 18th century, the introduction of a practical steam engine by James Watt helped usher in the industrial revolution in England. In the 1790s, the invention of the cotton gin by Eli Whitney would transform the economy of the South as well as the future of slavery.

In 1793, the director of the patent office was Thomas Jefferson, who also served as secretary of state. Whitney wrote to Jefferson that "with this Ginn, if turned with horses or by water, two persons will clean as much

The invention of the cotton gin increased cotton production greatly and is said to have extended the institution of slavery. Demand for cotton was suddenly great, thanks to the Industrial Revolution.

cotton in one Day, as a Hundred persons could cleane in the same time. . . ."[1]

After the cotton gin was introduced, it quickly began to revolutionize the economy of the South. Cotton production jumped from three thousand bales in 1790 to 178,000 bales in 1810. By 1860, the South was producing 4 million bales of cotton.[2] The invention of the cotton gin coincided with the dawning of the industrial revolution in England. The English had figured out a way to harness steam engines to power large looms. They wove cotton thread into cloth. The British manufacturers needed a steady supply of cotton. They found it in the American South. Southerners exported most of their cotton to England.

At first, the cotton was produced in states such as South Carolina and Georgia. But in 1803, President Thomas Jefferson acquired the vast Louisiana Territory from France. It included eight hundred thousand acres of land. Purchased for $15 million, the Louisiana Purchase almost doubled the size of the United States.

Suddenly, new lands became open to cotton cultivation. Cotton growing requires at least two

With the acquisition of the Louisiana Territory, the number of cotton plantations increased. There were vast amounts of land on which the crop could be planted, and slaves were needed to harvest it.

hundred days of weather in which the temperature remains above freezing. Much of the Louisiana Territory proved to be ideal for cotton. By 1834, the states of Alabama, Mississippi, and Louisiana, as well as the surrounding areas, were producing almost 300 million pounds of cotton. This was over half of all cotton produced in the United States.[3]

COTTON PLANTATIONS AND SLAVERY

Historian Peter Kolchin has pointed out that during the nineteenth century, plantations were usually much smaller than modern-day people envision. About 75 percent of all plantations had fewer than fifty slaves, with many having under ten. Plantation owners often worked side by side with the slaves in the fields. There was no need for an overseer. The owner managed the slaves. Only a tiny number of plantations, about one tenth of one percent, had two hundred slaves or more.[4]

By 1808, the United States government had outlawed the importation of slaves from Africa. Therefore, most of the slaves had to be supplied to the new cotton plantations from another source. Some came from plantations in the eastern states, such as Virginia and Maryland. Tobacco had removed most of the natural fertility of the soil. As a result, less and less tobacco could be grown. This meant that fewer and fewer workers were necessary.

Planters sold many of their slaves to slave traders. They transported them to the new southern states. Historians have estimated that over eight hundred thousand slaves were transported from the Chesapeake region, including Maryland and Virginia.[5] This was four times the number of slaves brought in by the Atlantic slave trade. Large traders operated in cities such as Richmond, Virginia, and Washington, DC. Once the slaves were sold, they were usually chained together. Then they were transported on foot, railroad, or boat to auctions in the deep South.

For many slaves, sale meant being separated from family and friends. Recalling his own sale, one slave wrote:

> We lay down on the naked floor to sleep in our handcuffs and chains. The women, my fellow slaves, lay on one side of the room; and the men who were chained with me, occupied the other…. I at length fell asleep, but was distressed by painful dreams. My wife and children appeared to be weeping and lamenting my calamity and beseeching and imploring my master on their knees not to carry me away from them.[6]

But it did no good—the slave was sold and taken from his family. Many of the slaves were taken to cities such as Memphis, Tennessee; Montgomery, Alabama; Natchez, Mississippi; and New Orleans, Louisiana. These were large slave trading centers. Here, the slaves were auctioned off to cotton and sugar planters or anyone else who needed them. As the demand for slaves grew, the prices of them increased. For example, a typical field hand who had sold for five hundred dollars in New Orleans in 1800 sold for eighteen hundred dollars in 1860. In Montgomery, a slave who had sold for eight hundred dollars in 1818 had doubled in price by 1860.[7] This meant that selling slaves could be very profitable for planters who no longer needed as many workers. Indeed, it became one of the primary ways that planters in the eastern southern states made money.

One planter outside of Savannah, Georgia, sold over four hundred slaves early in 1857. These included parents separated from their children, and brothers torn from their sisters. But the sale brought in the enormous sum of over $300,000. The planter needed the money to save his estates. He was about to lose them because of his habitual gambling.[8]

Slaves were sold in auctions to planters and agents. This degrading practice had the slave standing on a block, often partially naked, to be examined by buyers.

IN THE COTTON FIELDS

As one plantation owner wrote, "My creed as an agriculturist is to make the greatest possible product, from the least possible labor."[9] For a planter, this often meant having as few slaves as necessary. Then he wanted to get as much work out of them as he could to produce a substantial cotton harvest. By 1860, the majority of slaves in the South

Henry Clay Bruce described how much work he and his fellow slaves did on a typical harvest day at the plantation on which they worked.

We were called up by the overseer by means of a horn, ate breakfast and were in the field by daylight, sometimes, before it was light enough to see the cotton balls, and kept steadily at work till noon, when dinner was brought to us on large trays and the order given by the overseer to eat. We sat down right there and as soon as the last mouthful was swallowed the order was given to go to work. . . . From noon until dark we were driven by the overseer who carried a long whip called a blacksnake.

At dark, the females were allowed to go to their quarters, but the men and boys were divided into squads of five; each had a bale of cotton to turn out. Gins run by mules had been going all day, making lint cotton which had to be put in bales, and each bale had to stand under the press about twenty minutes, so that the last squad seldom got through earlier than nine o'clock; and this went on each day except Sunday.[10]

worked on plantations. The work varied, often depending on the ages of the slaves. As children, slaves often went into a master's house. Here, they cleaned, washed, and worked as personal servants. However, by the time a child reached adolescence, he or she frequently went to work in the cotton fields.

Growing cotton followed a cycle that repeated itself year after year. Early in the year, before spring began, slaves went to work with their hoes. They dug beds to plant the cotton seeds. Then holes were drilled. Seeds were placed into them and covered with soil. As the plants sprouted, the slaves continued hoeing. They removed any weeds from the cotton and thinned the rows of plants. Eventually, the cotton flowers sprouted. These were followed by the formation of pods. Finally, the white cotton appeared.

At harvest time, the cotton was picked. This was the hardest period of the year. The slaves had to bring in the cotton harvest before it could be destroyed by stormy weather. An adult slave was expected to pick about one hundred fifty pounds of cotton per day. But there were instances when that figure was more than doubled. The work was extremely hard. Slaves labored under the hot sun, with barely a break to eat. Older men were often bent double from years of hard labor. Their muscles ached; their feet hurt; and their fingers were raw from the thorns in the cotton plants. However, slaves were forced by their masters to work for as many hours as it took to get the job done.[11]

As one slave recalled:

> Grandma said slaves had to pick so many pounds of cotton a day, and they were given an awful whipping if they didn't get this amount. All the slaves who had fallen short had to stand in line with their backs bare for their whippin'. Grandma said that often she was whipped until she could barely grunt.[12]

After the harvest, the cotton had to be ginned. This is separating the seeds from the cotton lint, which is spun into cloth. One slave recalled:

Many perceived infractions would exact a whipping from a master or overseer. These could include something as serious as escaping to something as arbitrary as a glance, or for no reason at all.

"Ev'y night after work was over, us slaves had to gin cotton. 'Course dey had de gin machine, but it never wurked fas' as us [slaves] would pick de cotton, an' was always breakin'down. . . . Well, suh, ev'ybody had to gin a shoe full of cotton at night, fo goin' to bed."[13]

The workday began at sunrise and continued until sunset. Sometimes it lasted longer during the ginning season. Harvest time was the busiest period of the year. At other times, the pace was slower. In fact, during the heat of the summer, slaves might take a two-hour break during the middle of the ten-hour day. Frederick Law Olmsted, an architect from Hartford, Connecticut, traveled in the South during the 1850s. He reported conversations with plantation owners. They complained about the fact that slaves never worked very hard. One slave owner, he said, doubted that "they ever did half a fair day's work. They could not be made to work hard: they never would lay out their strength freely, and it was impossible to make them do it."[14] Of course, slaves had little reason to work hard. They did not get paid for their work. There were no bonuses if they picked more cotton. Nor could they expect to be promoted if they did an especially good job.

Indeed, some slaves tried to avoid work by pretending to be sick. Then they might be put in the "sick house" on a plantation.

Some slaves stayed there twenty days or more to avoid working. As Olmsted reported:

> I was on one plantation where a woman had been excused from any sort of labor for more than two years, on the supposition that she was dying. . . . At last [it was] discovered that she was employed as a milliner [hat maker] and dressmaker by all the other colored ladies of the vicinity. . . . She was hired out the next year to a fashionable dress-maker in town, at handsome wages. . . .[15]

OVERSEERS AND SLAVE DRIVERS

On large plantations, the owners generally employed managers such as overseers and slave drivers. The overseer supervised the day-to-day operations of a plantation. He was expected to enforce discipline among the slaves and make sure that they went to the fields and did their jobs properly. He directed slave gangs as they worked in the cotton fields. If any of the slaves were sick, he had to make sure that they were taken to the plantation hospital. The overseer was also responsible for the care of plantation animals. These might include cattle and sheep. They had to be well fed healthy to supply milk, meat, and wool to the people who lived on the plantation.

Only large plantations employed extra management like overseers and slave drivers. On smaller plantations, owners often worked alongside their slaves.

Overseers received little respect from planters. They constantly complained that most overseers never did a good job. In addition, the hours were often very long and the pay was low for the work they were expected to do. Overseers were regularly fired without warning by their employers.

As historian William Scarborough wrote:

> The overseer of a cotton plantation in the Lower South [Alabama, Louisiana and Mississippi] was given one year–if he were lucky– in order to prove his ability. If he did not harvest a bountiful crop during his initial year of service, he was likely to find himself looking for a new position the following year.[16]

Overseers often used brutal methods to bring in a good crop. They regularly whipped slaves in order to get them to work harder. On large plantations, slave drivers worked under overseers. These drivers also resorted to brutal treatment of slaves. As one plantation owner put it: "I rarely punish slaves myself, but make my driver virtually an executive officer to inflict punishments."[17] Drivers were slaves themselves. In South Carolina, plantation owner

James Henry Hammond's slave driver reported directly to him. Hammond was concerned that the overseer might not tell him about certain problems, like slaves who did not get all their work done. Therefore, Hammond wanted another source of information—his slave driver.[18]

Early in the morning, a driver would sound a horn to rouse the slaves and call them to breakfast. Then they were led into the fields to work. Under the supervision of a driver, a gang of slaves might be assigned to hoeing or plowing. Another gang might work on a roadway. Olmstead observed:

> We stopped for awhile, where some thirty men and women were at work, repairing the road. The women were in majority, and were engaged at exactly the same labor as the men; driving the carts, loading them with dirt, and dumping them upon the road,

cutting down trees, and drawing wood by hand, to lay across the miry [wet] places; hoeing and shoveling.[19]

Drivers called the slaves to stop work and break for lunch. Along with the overseers, the drivers were often responsible for livestock on the plantation. If a slave ran away, drivers might also participate in the effort to find him.

AT THE BIG HOUSE

Many slaves, male and female, worked in the master's house. Some slaves regarded this role as a privileged position. They often dressed better than the field hands. In addition, they had an opportunity to eat leftover food from the master's kitchen. This was usually better than the food prepared for the field workers. However, the house slaves were more closely supervised by the master and his family. Many field slaves did not want this kind of supervision, even if it meant better food and less backbreaking work.

House slaves did a variety of chores. These included cooking, cleaning, washing, and caring for children. They also had other duties. One slave recalled milking the plantation cows every morning. "We was up before five," she recalled, "and by five we better be in that cow pen. We better milk all of them cows too or they'd bull-whip us."[20] Another slave recalled that her mother did the washing in the master's house in a big tub. The water was heated in large kettles over a fire. Then the clothes were washed with soap made with lye, a strong, white powder.

Female slaves were also put to work on spinning wheels and looms. They were expected to make clothes for the master's family, as well as for other slaves.

HIRING OUT

Slave hiring was common on plantations during the nineteenth century. Slaves with special talents were made available to other plantations. This regularly happened if there was not enough work to keep slaves fully employed on their master's property. It was also another way for a slave owner to earn money on his slaves. The slaves worked in a variety of places. These included factories that processed tobacco, on steamboats, and in coal mining.

January 1 was usually hiring day. On that day, a slave was hired out for an entire year at a fixed price. This might be two hundred dollars for a field hand or as much as five hundred dollars for a blacksmith.[21]

Some slaves, however, did not like the idea of leaving their friends and family behind on the plantation. Once they were hired out, they might decide to run away from their new jobs and return home. One plantation owner related an incident to Frederick Law Olmsted, who was opposed to slavery and later designed New York's Central Park. The story was about a slave who had been hired out to work on the railroad. He ran away and was later caught and put in the local jail. There he pretended to be sick, the plantation owner said, "but after he had been in seven days, he all of a sudden said he'd got well, and he wanted something to eat. As soon as I heard of it, I sent them word to give him a good paddling, and handcuff him, and send him back to the rail-road."[22]

A slave was always expected to obey his or her master. This was the foundation of the slave system in the South.

CHAPTER 5

SLAVES AND MASTERS

James Henry Hammond, slaveholder and US Senator from South Carolina, stood on the Senate floor in 1858 and told his colleagues from the South and the North:

> In all social systems, there must be a class to do the menial duties, to perform the drudgery of life. That is, a class requiring but a low order of intellect and but little skill. . . . It constitutes the very mud-sill of society. . . . Fortunately for the South, she found a race adapted to that purpose to her hand. . . . We use them for our purpose, and call them slaves.[1]

Friction between the North and South had been growing over the issue of slavery for several decades. Some northerners wanted to abolish slavery. Many others wanted to prevent slavery from expanding to the new western territories. These had been acquired from Mexico as a result of the United States' victory in the Mexican War, which lasted from 1846 until 1848. Hammond spoke for most white southerners, who defended slavery. They generally regarded African Americans as inferior people. White southerners also wanted to see slavery expand to the new states being carved out of the West.

Yet slave owners like Hammond did not lose sight of another fact. As human beings, slaves had to be cared for by their owners. During the 1850s, Hammond wrote an elaborate manual. In it he gave detailed instructions for how slaves should be treated by their masters. For example, Hammond said that every male slave should receive two cotton shirts, a pair of woolen pants, and a woolen jacket in the fall. A woman received six yards of wool and the same amount of cotton. She was also given a needle and thread to make her own garments. Every worker also received four quarts of corn meal on Sunday, as well as a weekly supply of meat, usually pork.

Knowing that Hammond wanted to appear as humane as possible, slaves took advantage of the situation. Each year they received a holiday at Christmas time. One year, according to Hammond, they did not bring in a large harvest, and he wanted to reduce the length of their holiday.

Many plantations included slave hospitals, like the Melrose slave hospital in Louisiana, pictured here. Plantation owners needed to protect their investments by taking care of ill slaves.

However, Hammond said he "was persuaded out of my decision by [the] Negroes." He also claimed that they were "too well fed & otherwise well treated" than they deserved to be.[2]

Some slaves reported that their masters allowed them to have adequate food. But others found their food allotments barely adequate. They were regularly looking for more. Hammond's slaves stole his wine. Others took meat. ". . . we ain 'lowd to ever put our foot inside de meat house [where meat was smoked and cured]," one slave said. "Ole mistress kept de floor covered wid sawdus. . . . An' she better not find nary track in dat sawdus'. Anyhow my mother gwan in dere, but she ain' never fergit to rub out her tracks. We got meat an' my mother ain' got caught neither."[3]

Plantation owners also provided their slaves with cabins. These were often one-room houses built of wood. Some cabins had two rooms, for large families with many children. Each cabin had a fireplace where a slave family could cook its food. The chimney might be made of brick. However, chimneys were often made of mud and sticks that caught on fire. As a result, an entire cabin might be destroyed in flames.

The cabins had dirt floors and very little furniture. Slaves often slept on straw mattresses. The other furniture might include a few chairs and a table. There were also some cooking implements, like pots. One type of large frying pan was called a spider. In addition, there might be several gourds that the slaves used for drinking, as well as a wooden bucket for washing. Some cabins had no windows. Others might have a window protected by a shutter that could be closed over it, but no glass. This allowed insects to come into the cabin in the summer. The cold wind blew through the shutters and walls in winter. By contrast, the plantation owners often lived in large mansions, with magnificent furniture, glass at the windows, and plenty of fireplaces to warm them.

Because of poor living conditions, slaves might easily develop pneumonia or other diseases. However, many plantation owners tried to care for their slaves when they became sick. James Hammond, for example, ordered that slaves should be removed from their cabins and taken to the plantation hospital. He prescribed herbal medicines for the slaves. Hammond believed that a doctor was unnecessary for them.

REASONS TO CARE FOR SLAVES

Plantation owners like Hammond took care of their slaves for a variety of reasons. Among the most important was the fact that the slaves were expensive to buy and considered necessary for the plantation to produce large profits. As one southerner put it, slave owners kept their slaves healthy "to prolong the useful laboring period of a Negro's life."[4]

Thomas B. Chaplin, a cotton planter in South Carolina, kept a journal of his Tombee Plantation during the nineteenth century. When his slaves were sick, he was unhappy because they could not work. "This sickness is bad for me in getting out my crop," he wrote in 1849.[5] Chaplin also refused to let a slave get away with pretending to be sick.

As he wrote in 1850, "Helen had an idea of laying up today but I saw that nothing much was the matter and made her go out to work. I am determined to look more closely into their complaints, and not allow anyone to shirk from their work and sham sickness."[6]

However, some planters did feel real concern for their slaves. Owners regarded slaves as their responsibility. In Virginia, for example, one mistress hired out several of her slaves. She wanted to make sure that they would only go to work for masters who did not treat them cruelly.[7] Another master wanted to be certain that his slave was not hired out to the same hotel where he had worked in the past. He feared that the slave's health would not allow him to do the heavy work in the hotel. Other masters went so far as to let their slaves determine where they would hire out and work.[8]

They also wanted to show the rest of the United States that they were good masters. They reasoned that if slaves were treated well, there would be less reason for northerners to attack slavery. During the nineteenth century, more and more northerners were calling for slavery to be abolished. However, if they saw slaves being treated well and changed their views, they might leave the South alone. Then, slavery would continue to flourish.

James Henry Hammond was one of slavery's greatest champions. He realized that cotton planting was economically beneficial for the United States. Cotton was shipped north, where it was used in the mills of New England to manufacture cloth. Most importantly, cotton was also the largest US export. It brought in more money from sales abroad than the total of all other American goods.[9]

LAWS THAT CONTROLLED THE SLAVES

King cotton lived off the labor of slaves. From their earliest years, these slaves were taught to be subservient to their masters. They learned to bow their heads when speaking to the plantation owner or his wife. The owners, in turn, referred to every slave—no matter how old—as "boy" or "girl."

The lives of these slaves were tightly controlled by a series of state laws known as slave codes. In Louisiana, the code stated that "A slave is one in the power of a master to whom he belongs. The master may sell him, dispose of his person, his industry, and his labor; and he can do nothing, possess nothing, nor acquire anything but what must belong to his master."[10]

Slaves also lacked the other legal rights that adults enjoyed. They could not make contracts with people to buy and sell land. They owned no land. Slaves were prevented from traveling from one plantation to another without a written pass. It had to be signed by their master or the overseer. Each pass included the name of the slave, where he was going, and when he was supposed to return. In cities, slaves wore badges when they traveled away from their masters. Without these badges, they could immediately be stopped and sent home.

Slaves were strictly forbidden to read or write. White southerners feared that if slaves learned these skills, they could more easily communicate with each other on other plantations. They could also read about the freedom that black people had in the North. As a result, slaves might begin to join together and start a revolution. The slave code of Georgia, for example, expressly forbade anyone from teaching slaves to read or write. Slaves who tried to learn were punished by a fine, a whipping, and even risked being sold by their master.

Slaves were kept down by codes that forbade them to learn to read or write. Such a skill, it was believed, would only lead to trouble.

Nevertheless, some slaves did learn to read. As one slave recalled:

We had one smart slave on our plantation, Joe Sutherland, who was master's coachman. Joe always hung around the courthouse with master. He went on business trips with him, and through this way, Joe learned to read and write unbeknown to master. In fact, Joe got so good that he learned how to write passes for the slaves.[11]

Slave owners were especially concerned about slaves gathering together. They feared that these gatherings might be places where slaves could be plotting an insurrection. Whites were especially suspicious of religious gatherings. The Georgia slave code prohibited any religious exercise without a written certificate. In addition, no African American was permitted to preach without a license. Anyone who violated this law could be fined, whipped, or imprisoned.

Nevertheless, plantation owners believed that it was important for slaves to attend church. In many cases, however, this religious instruction was strictly controlled. As one slave recalled:

> Most times the white preacher would preach, then he would set . . . listenin' while the colored preacher preached. That was the law at that time. . . . [Slaves] had to set an' listen to the white man's sermon, but they didn' want to 'cause they knowed it by heart. Always took his text from Ephesians [part of the New Testament in the Bible], the white preacher did, the part what said, "Obey your masters, be good servant."[12]

Slaves routinely disobeyed their masters. They held their own services without permission. They found places in the woods to listen to their own preacher deliver a sermon. They read from the Bible and sang hymns. However, the slaves always risked that such a religious gathering might be discovered and broken up by the slave patrols.

Slaves were allowed to worship at church services, but the message was often meant to keep them in their place. They also held their own services.

THE ROLE OF SLAVE PATROLS

Since the colonial period, slave patrols had existed in the South. Their purpose was to control slaves and prevent them from violating the laws. In some states, such as Virginia and South Carolina, they were paid for their work. The patrols operated in the cities, as well as the country-side. In cities, such as Charleston, South Carolina, they checked slaves to make sure they wore badges while they traveled along the streets. Patrols also removed slaves who went to taverns and drank with their friends.

Throughout the South, the patrols tried to enforce the slave codes. Under the codes, for example, slaves could not travel in the countryside without a pass. They were prohibited from selling goods. If the patrol caught anyone violating these laws, the slaves could be hauled into jail. Slave patrols also tried to break up unlawful slave gatherings, including church ceremonies. One slave recalled that his friends used to station lookouts at these meetings. They gave a warning if the slave patrols were approaching. A lookout would whistle, and the other slaves would run for the woods.[13]

Slaves liked to trick the patrols, which they called patterrollers or paddyrollers. As one slave recalled:

> My father was once attending a prayer meeting in a house which had only one door. The slaves had turned a large pot down in the center of the floor to hold the sounds of their voices within. (No sounds can escape from a closed room, if a big pot [is] turned down in the middle of it.) But, despite their precaution, the patrols found them and broke in . . . my father stuck a big shovel in the fireplace, drew out . . . hot ashes and cinders and flung them . . . into the faces of [the] patrolers. The room was soon filled with smoke and . . . every Negro escaped.[14]

Slaves used other methods of dealing with the patrols. For example, they would put vines across roads in the dark to knock patrolmen off their horses. Outside Alexandria, Virginia, in 1840, slaves attacked a patrol. In the darkness, they jumped from behind the bushes, after the patrol had stopped. Then they beat the patrolmen with clubs.

Patrols tried to scare slaves even if they were carrying passes. They might say that the slave would be punished and sometimes even brutalize him. In addition, slave patrols had the power to enter a slave's cabin without notice and search it. If anything illegal was found there, such as reading material, then a slave could be severely punished.

HOW THE SLAVE CODES WERE ENFORCED

The slave codes were supposed to be strictly enforced. In practice, however, some masters were more lenient than others. James Henry Hammond, for example, permitted some slaves to read. Some masters barely used the whip to punish their slaves. If the master was kind, the slaves benefited. If he was cruel, they had to withstand the punishment.

The slave codes were often supposed to protect slaves from cruel masters. Sometimes the courts stepped in to provide this protection. Historian Ariela Gross cites a case in Mississippi in 1860. Slaves were not allowed to testify in court. However, a Mississippi judge allowed a statement to be read in court that was made by the slave to his master stating he was too sick to work. The court said that the slave's words were "presumed to be honest" and he should not be forced to work.[15] In other cases, however, the slave was not protected. Thomas Chaplin was asked to sit on a jury that was investigating a white owner charged with killing one of his slaves. The slave, Roger, was crippled, and his master had tied him up with a chain around his neck. Roger later choked to death. The jury decided that Roger's death had been accidental. However, Chaplin knew better. "The verdict should have been that Roger came to his death by inhumane treatment to him by his master," Chaplin wrote.[16]

However, Chaplin was not opposed to a slave being brutally punished and even killed if he was caught doing something illegal. In 1855, he wrote about a slave owner J. T. Harvey, who had killed one of his slaves. He had caught the slave stealing a watermelon from a neighbor's garden. Harvey was put in jail. "Don't think Harvey had any intention to kill the fellow," Chaplin wrote, "pity some more runaway rascals could not be killed."[17]

Many slaves were beaten mercilessly with whips, as well as other instruments. One slave recalled a master who heated up a pipe and burned the flesh of his slaves with it. Another slave reported that his master used a whipping as a public spectacle. It was a warning to other slaves that the same thing would happen to them if they did not behave exactly as the owners wanted them to.

Slaves never knew what to expect. As historian John Oakes has written: "Perpetual uncertainty was an unwavering constant of slavery. It was one of the master's most potent weapons and one of the greatest horrors of slave life."[18]

FIGHTING BACK

Some slaves resisted their masters. They committed small acts of disobedience. Masters would order their field hands to do certain types of work, only to find out that they had done something else. Was this deliberate? It is difficult to tell. Thomas Chaplin, the master of Tombee Plantation, recalled such an incident. He sent his slaves to fetch rails for fences. Instead, they brought him poles. At other times, they were tending weak plants instead of planting new seedlings.[19]

Some took more drastic action than simply pretending to be sick to avoid work. They might intentionally cut off fingers and toes, so they would be unfit for work. Some even shot themselves in the hand or the foot so they could not work in the fields. A few even committed suicide rather than submit themselves to slavery.[20]

Some slaves attacked their masters or the overseers of the plantation. Slave codes included severe penalties against slaves who used poison against their masters. But some slaves did. Newspaper articles also reported that slaves periodically stabbed or shot their masters. Sometimes the violence occurred when a slave was being whipped by

Many slaves would do anything to avoid their plight. Fugitive slave Margaret Garner killed two of her own children so that they could not be captured back into slavery.

an overseer. The pain would become so great that he would turn on an overseer and kill him. During the 1830s, a slave named Will was being punished by an overseer. Will simply walked away. The overseer took out a gun and shot Will in the back. As the overseer approached him, Will attacked him with a knife. Will stabbed him several times, and the overseer later died.

The slave codes were very clear on the fate of a slave who killed a white man. Will was found guilty by the jury and condemned to death.[21]

ESCAPING FROM THE PLANTATION

A common form of resistance among slaves was running away. In many cases, a slave would only leave the plantation for a short period of time. It was a relief from the constant work or the punishment for not doing the work to the master's liking. If the slave were an especially valuable hand and a good worker, the master might not even whip him when he returned.

Some slaves left the plantation and hid out for years in the woods. The Dismal Swamp in North Carolina was a favorite hiding place for many slaves. The area was hard to penetrate and infested with snakes and other animals. As a result, the slave patrols often let the runaway slaves remain there.

On one plantation, a female slave was criticized by her mistress. The slave struck her. The mistress threatened to have her beaten by the master when he returned from the fields. Instead, the female slave went to her husband, who helped her escape from the plantation. He found a cave in the woods. He brought a stove and furniture there. The couple lived in the cave for seven years. They raised a family and did not leave until the slaves were finally freed in the 1860s as a result of the Civil War.[22]

Another slave recalled that when he was six years old, his uncle, Charlie, ran away from the plantation. One day, Charlie was whipped repeatedly. Once when this occurred, Charlie struck back at the slave driver who was whipping him. Then Charlie ran away. The first time he was caught by the slave patrols. But Charlie ran away a second time. He reached Chicago with the help of an abolitionist. Then he left the United States and took a boat to Canada.[23]

FREEDOM IN THE NORTH

During the three centuries of slavery, a number of slaves were fortunate enough to escape to freedom. It was a highly dangerous undertaking. Slaves were forced to hide in swamps and woods. They might be attacked by animals. They could starve from lack of food. The slaves also had to outwit the slave patrols. The patrols tried to recapture the slaves and bring them back to the plantation to be beaten. The slaves could easily get lost as they tried to move north. Even if they reached the Ohio River—the boundary line between the slave and the free states—they might drown as they tried to swim across it.

However, some slaves were willing to risk anything to be free. As slave Henry Bibb wrote to his master after escaping to Canada:

> To be compelled to stand by and see you whip and slash my wife without mercy, when I could afford her no protection, not even by offering myself to suffer the lash in her place, was more than I felt it to be the duty of a slave husband to endure, while the way was open to Canada. My infant child was also frequently flogged.... for crying until its skin was bruised literally purple. This kind of treatment was what drove me from home and family, to seek a better home for them.[24]

Some slaves were assisted by free African Americans who lived in the South. Others received help from fellow slaves. One of these was Arnold Gragston, a slave from Kentucky. Born in 1840, he was taught to read and write on his master's plantation. His master also gave him the freedom to travel to other plantations.

On one of these journeys, he met a female slave who wanted to escape to freedom. Gragston decided to risk his own life and take her. He rowed the girl across the Ohio River. The river current was strong, Gragston recalled. He was also frightened of being caught by the slave patrols. However, he had been told to look for a light and row toward it. Gragston spotted the light. When he reached the northern bank of the river, he was met by other men who helped him. They took the girl to freedom.

This was the first of many trips that Gragston made to carry slaves to Ohio. From there, they journeyed north to New York and Canada. Eventually, Gragston decided to escape himself. Together with his wife, he rowed across the river and headed north to Detroit, Michigan.[25]

Arnold Gragston was a member of the Underground Railroad. This was an escape network that brought slaves out of the South into the free states of the North, as well as Canada. From 1810 to 1850, an estimated one hundred thousand slaves were brought out of the South by the Underground Railroad. It was not an actual railroad, but a series of trails and hiding places that led north. These "stations," as they were called, were run by "conductors." They gave the slaves food to eat and a place to hide until they could be on their way.

Sometimes slaves would escape on their own. Some, however, were escorted by "conductors," like Gragston. They usually traveled at night. They followed the North Star in the heavens, to take them due North to the free states. They hid during the day at a station. Word was then passed to the next station to expect the fugitive slaves after another night's journey.

In 1850, Congress passed the Fugitive Slave Bill. This made it a crime for northerners to harbor escaped slaves. The South sent bounty hunters north to re-capture these slaves and return them to their masters. As a result, the Underground Railroad took many slaves into Canada or the Caribbean, where slavery had been abolished. There they could be safe from the Fugitive Slave Law of the United States.

As risky as it was, slaves continued to try to get away from the prison of the plantation. Many were aided to safety up north by station agents of the Underground Railroad.

REBELLION!

Some slaves were convinced that the only way to achieve freedom was to lead a revolt and throw off the power of their white masters. Such a rebellion was planned by an African American named Denmark Vesey. He was a member of the African Methodist Episcopal Church in Charleston, South Carolina. Vesey had purchased his freedom with the money he won in a lottery. In 1817, he preached to the slaves who attended the church. Vesey quoted passages about freedom from the Bible. He spoke to the people about throwing off the bonds of slavery. The Charleston city government feared that the church might be a center of revolution and arrested many of its members. Finally, in 1821, the church was closed. But by that time, Vesey had organized his revolution. Before it was launched, however, the Charleston authorities found out about it from a slave. Vesey and his associates were arrested and hanged in 1822.

As a result of the conspiracy, the slave codes were tightened in South Carolina. Free blacks who had left the state were not allowed to return. Federal troops were also stationed in Charleston. The city was heavily defended against another attempted rebellion.

Although Charleston was secure, another revolt occurred in Virginia. This uprising was led by a slave named Nat Turner. Born in 1800, Turner was permitted by his master to attend church, where he learned to read. He became a preacher. Turner related the visions he had experienced. In these visions, the powers of good and evil battled against each other.

Turner believed that he had been called to lead a slave revolt against the plantation owners. This was the power of good being led against the evil of the slave masters. He began the revolt on August 22, 1831. Turner and his followers attacked nearby plantations and slaughtered the white families there. However, the plantation owners rapidly assembled a force to put down the rebellion. Turner escaped into the woods, where he lived in a cave for several weeks. Eventually, he was caught and hanged on November 11, 1831.

An anonymous author tried to explain some of the reasons for the rebellion by Denmark Vesey in 1822.

REFLECTIONS, OCCASIONED BY THE LATE DISTURBANCES IN CHARLESTON, 1822
Previous to the proposal of any plan for preventing the recurrences of similar danger, it may be useful to advert to the causes which produced the late conspiracy. The following may be assigned as some of the most obvious:...The indiscreet zeal in favor of universal liberty, expressed by many of our fellow-citizens in the States north and east of Maryland; aided by the black population of those states....The idleness, dissipation, and improper indulgencies permitted among all classes of the Negroes in Charleston, particularly among the domestics: and, as the most dangerous of those indulgencies, their being taught to read and write: the first bringing the powerful operation of the Press to act on their uniformed and easily deluded minds; and the latter furnishing them with an instrument to carry into execution the mischievous suggestions of the former....[26]

This was the last slave revolt in the South. White southerners had many advantages that enabled them to defeat a slave revolt. Most important, whites had far more weapons than the slaves. Southerners could immediately form a small volunteer army to track down the

African-American rebels. On the other hand, the slaves had very few weapons. If they were found to possess them, they would be immediately punished by their masters. In addition, the slaves had difficulty planning a rebellion. They did not live together in large communities. Instead, groups of slaves lived on separate plantations. It was not easy for them to communicate with each other to plan a revolt. Any gathering of slaves might be broken up by the slave patrols. As a result, there were very few slave revolts in the South.

CHAPTER 6

CULTURE AND SLAVE LIFE

There are words like Freedom
Sweet and wonderful to say.
On my heartstrings freedom sings
All day everyday.

There are words like Liberty
That almost make me cry
If you had known what I know
You would know why.
—Langston Hughes, *The Panther and the Lash*

Although the plantation system was harsh, the lives of the slaves were not completely controlled. Slaves created a rich family life. Families gave the slaves support to deal with the harsh realities of slavery.

Slaves began courting when they were still adolescents. Courtship often occurred between slaves who lived on the same plantation. Over several generations, as slaves courted and married each other, they linked together many families. Sometimes, they created an extended community on a single plantation. Slaves also courted each other on neighboring plantations. Frequently, the men traveled on a Saturday night when the week's work was over. Marriages between slaves from different plantations created a large extended family network.

Marriages between slaves were not legally recognized by the Southern states. African Americans even needed the permission of their masters to unofficially "marry." Some marriage ceremonies were very simple. A plantation owner might simply read a few religious passages, usually from the Bible. In some ceremonies, a couple would simply jump over a broomstick to signify that they were married. But other ceremonies were far more elaborate. A slave recalled that at one marriage, the bride was dressed in white and wore a veil. She was accompanied by her best friends, who served as bridesmaids. The groom wore checked pants and a colorful coat. First the bride and then the groom marched down the center aisle of a church. They were married by a preacher. The ceremony was followed by an elaborate reception with food and banjo music.[1]

Slave marriages were not legally recognized because the slaves were not free to consent. Many slaves married nonetheless, ending their wedding ceremonies by "jumping the broom."

SLAVES AND THEIR FAMILIES

Slave children were frequently delivered by enslaved African-American midwives. These were often older women who had experience with childbirth. Once a woman gave birth to a child, she was expected to return to work. Slave children spent their infancy in a nursery. This was sometimes run by an older female slave. Mothers were frequently permitted to visit the nursery at regular times throughout the day to nurse their infants. But, in other cases, women worked at long distances from the nursery. The babies were brought to the fields to be nursed. After nursing, they might be laid in a cool shady place. They might also be carried by the slave women on their backs as they worked.

In the evenings, older children might help their parents wash clothes, cultivate the slave gardens, or do some sewing. Children also learned the songs and stories, which they heard from their parents or grandparents. As one slave recalled: "We worked hard in de field all day, but when dark come we would all go to de quarters and after supper we would set around and sing and talk."[2] In some cases, one person led the singing while others responded. Other songs were sung in unison. Because

Slaves were permitted to have children, but these offspring were considered property of the slaveowner. Many families were split up when slave children were sold to another plantation.

slaves weren't allowed to learn to read or write, they used a dialect, or variety, of English:

> 'Possum meat is good an' sweet,
> I always finds it good to eat.
> My dog tree, I went to see.
> A great big 'possum up dat tree.
> I retch up an' pull him in,
> Den dat ole 'possum 'gin to grin.[3]

In the evenings, children listened as their elders told stories. These might feature biblical characters, such as Moses leading the Jews out of slavery in Egypt. Other stories presented elements of African history to children who had never lived there. Slaves also told fables and folk tales, often featuring a wily animal who outwitted his enemies. These animals symbolized the slaves themselves. The message was clear: If a slave was smart enough, he or she might figure out a way to escape from the plantation. He or she might also be able to lead other slaves out of bondage and into freedom.

SPECIAL CELEBRATIONS

Although slaves worked hard for their masters, they also had time to enjoy special celebrations. Saturday nights were usually festive occasions. Some slaves were especially good singers and dancers who would entertain the others. But, just as often, all the slaves would participate in the singing and dancing. Especially popular were dances such as the "Turkey Trot." The slaves would gath-

In their off hours, slaves found joy and relaxation by singing, dancing, telling stories, and reciting Bible verses.

er in a cabin, remove the furniture, and form a ring. Then they would begin dancing to the music of fiddles and banjos, as a caller sang out the steps: "sashay to the right," "do-si-do," and "swing your partners."4

On Saturday nights, slaves might be permitted to visit neighboring plantations. This was especially important for families who were separated. That is, a man and his wife might work on different plantations. A male slave was given a pass so he could visit his wife and children. At least for the next twenty-four hours, they could live together as a family.

On Sundays, the slaves attended church. This was another opportunity to sing. Many of the spirituals were sung loudly by slaves who felt that they had been filled by the spirit of God. Slave owners thought that the Christian religion encouraged slaves to accept their fate. With its teaching of another existence beyond the grave, Christianity seemed to hold out the promise of a better life after death. Nevertheless, slaves fervently believed that their masters were committing a sin by keeping people in slavery.

After the church service, the slaves often participated in games that might include wrestling and boxing matches. Sometimes, there was a large dinner prepared by the slaves followed by singing and dancing.

One of the most festive times of the year was corn husking, or shucking, in the fall. As a slave recalled:

> You have two captains and they each choose the ones they want on their side. Then the shucking begins. The last one I attended, the side I was on beat by three barrels. We put our Captain on our shoulders and rode him up and down while everybody cheered and clapped their hands like the world was coming to an end. The shucking was followed by a large feast and dancing through the night.5

Another special time of the year was Christmas. Slaves were usually given a holiday that began just before Christmas and lasted until after

On the plantation where Annie L. Burton was enslaved, the young children did not get too much food since they did not have to work in the fields:

The slaves got their allowance every Monday night of molasses, meat, corn meal, and a kind of flour called "dredgings" or "shorts." Perhaps this allowance would be gone before the next Monday night, in which case the slaves would steal hogs and chickens. Then would come the whipping-post. Master himself never whipped his slaves; this was left to the overseer.

We children had no supper, and only a little piece of bread or something of the kind in the morning. Our dishes consisted of one wooden bowl, and oyster shells were our spoons. This bowl served for about fifteen children, and often the dogs and the ducks and the peafowl had a dip in it. Sometimes we had buttermilk and bread in our bowl, sometimes greens or bones.[6]

the New Year. However, plantation owners were especially watchful during the Christmas season. It was a long vacation and slaves joined together in large groups. Therefore, they might have a greater opportunity to plan activities against white slave owners. Slaves might decide to run away or start revolts. Therefore, the slave patrols were instructed to watch the roads and the countryside carefully.

Louisa Corbaux del. et lith.

EVA AND TOPSY.

"I love you because you haven't had any Father, or Mother, or Friends.—
because you've been a poor abused child!

Vide "Uncle Toms Cabin"

With few other children around, slave children were often play-
mates with the plantation owner's children. This changed as the
children grew up.

COMING OF AGE

Slaves often recalled living relatively carefree lives as children until they were four or five years old. They were regularly raised with the white children of the plantation owner. As one slave put it, "I grew up with the young masters. I played with them, ate with them and sometimes slept with them. We were pals. Because of my unusual strength and spirit I would let none of them beat me at any game or in any wrestle. I was the best of the young boys on the plantation." But all this changed as the slave grew. Then slaves were separated from whites. Slaves were also taught that they were expected to show obedience to their masters. As this slave added: "One day the old master carried me in the barn and tied me up and whipped me 'cause I wouldn't call my young masters, 'masters.'"[7]

This was not the only lesson that a young slave would learn. He was taught how to bow his head and take off his hat in the presence of the master or mistress of the plantation. He also learned to address them with great respect. A young slave came to realize that his father or mother could not save him from a beating by the plantation owner if he misbehaved. Indeed, a man could not even protect his own wife from a beating. This must have been especially difficult for a man who was also a husband and a father.[8]

Some masters forced their attentions on the slave women whom they owned. These women generally had no choice but to submit. South Carolina slave owner James Henry Hammond, for example, had intimate relationships with two of his slaves.[9] According to one estimate there were almost a quarter of a million slaves by 1850 who had been born to white men

87

and black slaves. Historian John Hope Franklin wrote that some plantation owners took special care of their children. In some cases, they were even freed. But other masters were not so kindly. They did not hesitate to sell them, as they would any other slave.[10]

SELLING OFF FAMILY MEMBERS

Sale was the threat that hung over every slave family member. Some slaves were fortunate. Their owners did not believe in breaking up a family. But other owners were not so considerate. An owner might be in need of money. Although he might not want to break up a family, he might believe there was no other choice. As Thomas Chaplin, the owner of the Tombee Plantation wrote:

> I never thought that I would be driven to this very unpleasant extremity. Nothing can be more mortifying and grieving to a man than to select out some of his Negroes to be sold. You know not to whom, or how they will be treated by their new owners. And Negroes that you find no fault with—to separate families, mothers & daughters, brothers & sisters—all to pay for your own extravagances.[11]

Although Chaplin said he felt badly, he sold the slaves, nevertheless.

Historians estimate that about one-fifth of all slave marriages were broken up due to sales.[12] Indeed, from the time they were children, slaves were told that the break up of their families was a distinct possibility. Frequently, slaves differentiated between a "good" master and a "bad" one based on whether they would consider breaking up a family by sale. In some cases, slaves were sold following the death of their master. For example, after the death of Thomas Jefferson in 1826, his estate at Monticello in Virginia was $100,000 in debt. To pay off this debt, equivalent to $10 million at today's prices, his slaves were sold. There were over one hundred thirty of them. Some of the slaves sold for as much as four hundred dollars, while others sold for as little as fifty dollars.[13] At the auction, families were separated so the debt could be paid.

For these slave families, and many others just like them across the South, the sales were tragic. Fathers were often separated and sold from the rest of their families. This is one of the reasons why some of the families on plantations were raised by single parents. One slave recalled that after her father was sold, he would secretly return at night to see his children. They would sit on his lap and hug him. But this came at a price: he was often caught and beaten by his master for leaving the plantation.[14]

Some slaves tried to stay in touch with their families after being sold. Most slaves could not read or write. However, they would have a white master or mistress write a letter for them. Then it was sent off to the plantation where a loved one had been sold. In this way, some contact continued, even though the families might be separated by many miles and several states.

SLAVE LIFE IN THE CITIES

While slave in the cities lived under the control of their masters, everyday life was different. In part, this was because the slaves had different work to do and lived under different conditions. Writing about the southern cotton factories he visited, a man from England said:

> In each of them are employed from 80 to 100 persons, and about an equal number of white and black. In one of them, the blacks are the property of the mill-owner, but in the other two they are the slaves of planters, hired out at monthly wages to work in the factory. There is no difficulty among them on account of color, the white girls working in the same room and at the same loom with the black girls.[15]

Some slaves preferred city life to work on a plantation. In Galveston, Texas, for example, one slave owner reported that a slave he purchased "has Sworned not to work on any planta-tion and says he will not live out of a city of town." There was more social life in towns, and it was more difficult for owners to con-trol their slaves. They often lived in their own houses because there was no room in the homes of their masters. However, these houses were little more than shacks. Nevertheless, slaves gathered regularly at their homes where they drank, smoked and gambled.

Slaves were permitted to attend large dances, supervised by white owners. In Galveston, there were also separate churches permitted for black slaves. While slave owners passed laws to restrict slaves, similar to those on plantations, it was much harder to enforce these laws in towns. Slaves could more easily escape the attention of whites and enjoy more freedom.[16]

When the United States capital was built in Washington DC during the late 18th and 19th centuries, slaves did most of the work. Barefoot men, women and children, wearing little more than torn clothing, hauled stones out of the swamps to be used for buildings. Skilled male slaves chiseled the stones and used their expertise to cut lumber that was used in the White House and the Capital buildings. These slaves were paid $5 per month by the federal government.

One of these slaves was Philip Reid, whose owner, a Maryland sculptor, made

The stately US Capitol was built in part by slaves rented out by their owners. The capitol now features a plaque commemorating the contributions of enslaved African Americans to the building.

A letter to the commissioner of public buildings, marble quaries May 16, 1817, describes the difference between city and plantation life.

The employ of the plantation negroes is not by any means so fatiguing and laborious, as those employed here; they can generally find conveniency to Skulk, more or less at their respective jobbing about a plantation; a thing entirely out of the question here where every negroe is under the eye of the superintendent....Added to this the work is of the most fatiguing kind; diffing, Shoveling & whelling dirt, tumbling large pieces of the Rock, where every muscle of the body must be strained, boring holes, and driving wedges, & Tongs with heavy Sledges; indeed the handling of the bits, sledges, crowbars, drills...is heavy work of itself, and requires a constant exertion of muscular power.[17]

the Statue of Freedom that rises over the Capital. Philip had the skill to take apart the plaster molds, so they could be moved separately to a foundry and cast into iron. He was also in charge of the casting and was paid $1.25 on Sunday "keeping up fires under the moulds," on the day when no work was done. That way, the fires would not have to be started again on Mondays. In 2010, these slaves finally received recognition from the US government with a series of plaques commemorating their work.[18]

CHAPTER 7

EMANCIPATION

The 1860 election of Republican Abraham Lincoln as president brought America to the breaking point. Lincoln was opposed to the expansion of slavery into the western territories. And many Southerners took that to mean that the days of their slave-based economy were numbered. Thomas Chaplin, the owner of Tombee Plantation in South Carolina and some of his friends talked openly about secession at a luncheon in the fall. One of the men at the luncheon compared secession to "a second Declaration of Independence." If the South established its own government, then planters could control the slaves without any criticism from the abolitionists of the North.[1]

One month later, South Carolina became the first state to secede from the Union. It was followed by ten other states. The new Confederate States of America, as it was called, established its capital in Montgomery,

Alabama. Elected president of the Confederacy was Jefferson Davis, a former United States Senator and a Mississippi plantation owner.

On April 12, 1861, Confederate troops in Charleston Harbor fired on the Union position at Fort Sumter. Federal forces surrendered the next day. The opening of the Civil War was greeted with great joy by many southerners. Like Chaplin, they believed that only independence would enable them to preserve their way of life. However, the war soon began to take an entirely different direction. It led to the end of the plantation system and freedom for four million slaves.

THE BEGINNING OF A NEW LIFE

Slaves quickly learned about the war. Indeed, some of them were forced by Confederate forces to build fortifications. These were used to protect southern harbors against possible invasion by northern troops. Instead of completing their work, some slaves fled. They headed north to Union positions in northern Virginia. These refugees were still legally slaves. But the Union commanders did not return them to their owners. They were given jobs, similar to those that they had been doing for the Confederate forces. African- American women and children also began leaving nearby plantations. They were taken into the Union lines. In August 1861, the US Congress passed the Confiscation Act. This stated that any escaping slaves who had been employed by the Confederacy in war work could remain with Union forces.

In November 1861, Union forces launched a successful invasion of the South Carolina coast. Chaplin and other plantation owners were driven off their lands. These plantations were taken over by the Federal government. They were worked by African Americans who had been slaves. They were paid to grow cotton that would be used to manufacture clothing for the Federal troops. In addition, the African-American farmers planted corn to feed themselves.

During 1862, Union forces advanced more deeply into the South. As word of this advance reached the plantation slaves, their reactions were mixed. Some slaves remained on the plantations and continued to work for their white masters. One slave named Cato recalled that his master joined the Confederate Army. Cato was told by his master to protect the plantation and the women who lived there. He even carried a gun to guard the fields and the main house. He prevented anyone from stealing anything.[2]

However, some plantation owners reported that relations between the slaves and their masters had changed. Slaves reportedly did not work as hard. They only did what they wanted, not what they were ordered to do. Many plantation owners had left to enlist in the Confederate Army. This left their wives to run the plantations. They lacked the power to achieve as much obedience from the slaves. Often they had to rely on overseers to enforce discipline. But the South needed all able-bodied men in the armed forces. This included overseers who were required to serve in the Confederate Army.

Many slaves saw an opportunity to flee the plantations. They left to seek refuge with the Union Army. Male slaves frequently came in on their own. They wanted to find out what the conditions would be like in the Union camp. They had been told by Southerners that the Union commanders imprisoned the slaves. They found out that this was not true. Then they often went back to the plantations and helped their wives and children to escape. Entire families made their way to the Union camps.

Federal commanders welcomed the male slaves. They often proved invaluable as scouts. They knew local roads and trails and could direct Union forces against Confederate positions. The women and children were harder to care for. They congregated in refugee camps, where conditions were terrible. One Union officer reported that "the suffering from hunger & cold is so great that those wretched people are dying by scores—that sometimes thirty per day die & are carried out by wagon loads, without coffins, & thrown . . . like brutes, into a trench. . . ."[3] Union armies were trying to carry on a war. They simply did not focus on the needs of the refugee slaves.

Nevertheless, these refugees slowly began to have an impact on the course of the Civil War. Historian Ira Berlin has pointed out that the

Male slaves proved invaluable to the Union. Here, an African American work crew in northern Virginia provides service for the Union Military Railway Service.

war began as an effort to hold together the Union. Abraham Lincoln did not want to talk about emancipating the slaves. He feared alienating border states, such as Missouri and Kentucky. There were many slaveholders in these states. Lincoln was afraid that the slaveholders might lead their states into the Confederacy, if he announced an intention to free the slaves. However, the presence of the slaves in the Union camps made it impossible to ignore the issue. Gradually, African-Americans helped to change the war's focus.[4]

Finally, on January 1, 1863, the president issued the Emancipation Proclamation. This document set free all the slaves in the states that were still in rebellion against the United States.

African American soldiers of Connecticut's 29th Regiment perform a drill in South Carolina in 1864. Former slaves served in both the Union and the Confederate armies.

THE SOUTHERN RESPONSE

At first, the southern plantation owners ignored the Emancipation Proclamation. As Union troops continued their invasion of the southern states, the planters tried to prevent their slaves from fleeing to the Federal lines. These slaves were carried into the interior, where the Union had not yet appeared. Often, only old men and sick slaves were left on the plantations. One government official reported that when he arrived at a plantation, the old African Americans had been left to fend for themselves. They lived in broken-down houses that were dirty and had no furniture.[5]

Other slaves were forced to serve the Confederate cause. Some worked in the Tredgar Iron Works, located in Richmond, Virginia. The iron works made cannon and other armaments used by the Confederate soldiers. Other slaves mined iron that was needed for the war effort. Still others served in the Confederate Army. They worked as cooks, dug fortifications, carried litters with wounded soldiers, and built campsites. The Confederacy did not want to arm the slaves and put them in the battle lines. There was too much fear that if the slaves were armed, they would revolt. However, as the war neared its end, the Confederate Congress debated whether to arm the slaves. Finally, in March 1865, they agreed that slaves should be armed. By that time, however, the Civil War was lost.

Meanwhile, slaves who escaped the South served on the battlefield for the Union. Approximately, 180,000 African-Americans served in Federal army units.[6] About one half were former slaves from the Confederate states. Some of these African Americans marched onto plantations, where they freed the slaves who were still left working in the fields. Other slaves, however, did not learn of their freedom until the war had ended in April 1865.

In many parts of the South, the former slaves greeted the news of their freedom with celebrations. In Charleston, for example, thousands of slaves crowded into the streets. They were singing and cheering. Some of the former slaves sang:

'Tain't no mo' sellin' today,
'Tain't no mo' hirin' today
'Tain't no pullin' off shirts today,
Its stomp down freedom today.
Stomp it down![7]

FREEDOM AND CHANGE

Freedom brought change for African Americans. Some of it was positive and some of it negative. In 1865, Congress passed—and the states ratified—the Thirteenth Amendment to the Constitution, which formally

May 11th, 1867

Chief of the Freedmen's Bureau at Richmond;

Dear Sir,

I am anxious to learn about my sisters, from whom I have been separated many years. I have never heard from them since I left Virginia twenty four years ago. I am in hopes that they are still living and I am anxious to hear how they are getting on. I have no other one to apply to but you and am persuaded that you will help one who stands in need of your services as this. I shall be very grateful to you if you oblige me in this matter. One of my sisters belonged to Peter Coleman in Caroline County and her name was Jane. Her husband's name was Charles and he belonged to Buck Haskin and lived near John Wright's store in the same county. She had three children, Robert, Charles and Julia, when I left. Sister Martha belonged to Dr Jefferson, who lived two miles above Wright's store. Sister Matilda belonged to Mrs. Botts, in the same county. My dear uncle Jim had a wife at Jack Langley's and his wife was named Adie and his oldest son was named Buck and they all belonged to Jack Langley. These are all my own dearest relatives and I wish to correspond with them with a view to visit them as soon as I can hear from them. My name is Hawkins Wilson and I am their brother who was sold at Wright's sale and

After the war, many former slaves set about attempting to reunite with their scattered family members. This letter was sent to the Freedman's Bureau by a man hoping to locate his sisters.

The Freedman's Bureau established schools throughout the South to educate African American children. This photo shows freed slave children with their teachers.

freed the slaves. As the Civil War ended, many former slaves decided to legalize their marriages. In one part of Virginia, for example, over fifty percent of African-American couples legally registered their marriages. In several areas of North Carolina, approximately forty-seven percent of African-American couples did the same thing.[8] Many couples were also "re-married" by a priest or minister.

Historians believe that these efforts by African Americans demonstrate the strength of the black family.[9] These families had survived during slavery. They were also strengthened by African Americans following the Civil War.

Some slave families who had been broken apart by plantation owners made an effort to reunite after the end of the war. African Americans worked through the Freedmen's Bureau. This organization had been established by the Federal Government in 1865 to help the freed slaves. One woman asked the Bureau to help her find her five children who had been sold before the war. The Bureau brought the woman and one child together and found some information on two of her other children. But the last two were never discovered.[10]

The Freedmen's Bureau also set up schools in the South for African Americans to attend. Over forty-three hundred schools were established by the Freedmen's Bureau. These included Fisk University, Hampton Institute, and Howard University. Other schools were established by African Americans themselves. Both adults and children attended these schools. They hoped to make up for years of neglect, when they had not been permitted to learn how to read or write.

This tale of emancipation was told by ex-slave Nat Love in his autobiography. Love went on to become a famous cowboy.

Finally Lee surrendered and master returned home. But in common with other masters of those days he did not tell us we were free. And instead of letting us go he made us work for him the same as before, but in all other respects he was kind. He moved our log cabin on a piece of ground on a hill owned by him, and in most respects things went on the same as before the war. It was quite a while after this that we found out we were free and good news, like bad news, sometimes travels fast. It was not long before all the slaves in the surrounding country were celebrating their freedom. And "Massa Lincoln" was the hero of us all.

While a great many slaves rejoiced at the altered state of affairs; still many were content to remain as before, and work for their old masters in return for their keep. My father, however, decided to start out for himself, to that end he rented twenty acres of land, including that on which our cabin stood, from our late master.[11]

In addition to education, African-American churches also flourished after the end of the war. African-American Baptists organized their own church. Meanwhile, the African Methodist Episcopal Church almost quadrupled its membership to seventy-five thousand by 1866.[12]

While some aspects of African-American life improved, others did not. Many Southerners resented the fact that slaves had been set free as a result of the Civil War. They vowed to keep African Americans in an inferior position. Southern states passed a series of laws, known as Black Codes. These were designed to limit the freedom of the former slaves.

Under the Codes, freed slaves were considered vagrants if they did not have jobs and could be sent to prison. Apprentice laws declared that if an African American was considered unfit to care for his children, they could be taken away. Then they could be hired out to a white employer. This was an attempt by whites to take back the workers that they had lost when slavery ended. Eventually, the Freedmen's Bureau put a stop to this practice. Other elements of the Black Codes stated that blacks could not testify against whites in court, or carry any weapons.

In 1866, Congress passed the Civil Rights Act to counter the Black Codes. This act stated that African Americans were entitled to the same rights as any other citizen. These rights were later confirmed by the Fourteenth Amendment to the Constitution. It was passed by Congress later in 1866. This Amendment guaranteed that African Americans had the right to vote and hold political office.

Nevertheless, the antagonism of whites against blacks did not disappear in the South. In 1865 and 1866, approximately five thousand African Americans were murdered. In Memphis, Tennessee, African-American churches and schools were set on fire in 1866. A race riot in New Orleans left thirty-four African Americans dead.

FREE, YET NOT FREE

What African Americans had hoped for as a result of freedom was a way to make a living. For many, this meant land to farm. But they did not receive any land. Many African Americans found themselves working for wages on the same land where they had worked as slaves. Men earned a low wage, nine dollars to fifteen dollars per month, and women were paid even less.[13] Other former slaves found themselves working as sharecroppers. They leased land from their former owners

Some former slaves took advantage of Homestead Acts enacted by the government. The laws gave African Americans ownership of land at little or no cost.

and received some of the money for the cotton crop each year. This was considered an improvement over slavery. At least the African-American sharecroppers could not be sold to other farms. Their families could not be broken apart.

However, contracts between the African Americans and the farm owners were not written. Some slaves complained that the owners tried to cheat them out of their rightful share of the crops. In addition, the farm owners often set up stores where sharecroppers bought tools, food, and other supplies. These necessities were paid on credit until a crop was harvested. The farm owners often charged high rates of interest. Consequently, the African-American sharecroppers found themselves deep in debt.

In 1866, the Southern Homestead Act was passed giving any head of a family eighty acres of Federal lands for five dollars. Some African Americans took advantage of this opportunity to obtain land in Florida, Arkansas, Alabama, Mississippi, and Louisiana. Others were fortunate enough to have saved a little money. They bought land in other parts of the South. But the majority of African Americans remained tied to the land of their former owners. As one African American put it:

> We knowed freedom was on us, but we didn't know what was to come with it. We thought we was goin' to get rich like white folks . . . 'cause we was stronger and knowed how to work, and the whites didn't and they didn't have us to work for them anymore. But it didn't turn out that way. We soon found out that freedom could make folks proud but it didn't make 'em rich.[14]

Plantation life had left African Americans with little knowledge of what to expect when freedom came. The brutal plantation system had prevented slaves from learning to read and write, owning property, or living independent lives. Plantation life had lasted for more than two centuries. Once it was over, blacks began to walk the long road toward achieving equality with white Americans in education, employment, and standards of living.

TIMELINE

1619 Africans arrive in Jamestown, Virginia. 1664 Maryland orders slaves to remain in bondage until death.

1674 The Royal Africa Company is established, imports slaves to New World.

1740s The religious revival known as the Great Awakening begins.

1750 Forty thousand slaves live in South Carolina and Georgia.

1775–1781 American Revolution; at least 40,000 slaves run away from plantations.

1787 At the Constitutional Convention, international slave trade is banned by 1808.

1793 Eli Whitney invents the cotton gin.

1800 Gabriel Prosser leads an unsuccessful slave revolt.

1803 The United States makes the Louisiana Purchase; cotton production expands westward.

1808 International slave trade is ended.

1810–1850 Slaves are brought to freedom on the Underground Railroad.

<u>1811</u> A slave revolt in New Orleans suppressed.

<u>1821</u> Denmark Vesey leads an unsuccessful slave revolt.

<u>1831</u> Nat Turner's slave revolt is put down.

<u>1860</u> The slave population stands at four million.

<u>1861–1865</u> The North and South fight Civil War.

<u>1863</u> President Abraham Lincoln issues the Emancipation Proclamation.

<u>1865</u> Congress passes the Thirteenth Amendment, formally freeing all slaves and outlawing slavery; the Freedmen's Bureau is established.

<u>1866</u> Congress passes the Fourteenth Amendment, extending civil rights to African Americans.

CHAPTER NOTES

CHAPTER 1. SLAVERY AMID FREEDOM

1. Yuval Taylor, ed., *I Was Born a Slave: An Anthology of Classic Slave Narrative* (Chicago, IL: Lawrence Hill Books, 1999), vol. 1, p. 191.
2. William Grimes, "Life of William Grimes, the Runaway Slave, Brought Down to the Present Time: Electronic Edition," *University of North Carolina at Chapel Hill Libraries: Documenting the American South*, © 2000, http://docsouth.unc.edu/neh/grimes55/grimes55.html (December 2, 2003).
3. Taylor, p. 192.
4. Ibid., p. 220.
5. Ibid., vol. 2, p. 490.
6. Ibid., p. 491.

CHAPTER 2. THE BEGINNINGS OF SLAVERY

1. Paul Finkelman, ed., *Colonial Southern Slavery* (New York, NY: Garland Publishing, 1989), p. xii.
2. Hugh Thomas, *The Slave Trade* (New York, NY: Simon and Schuster, 1997), pp. 114, 185.
3. Mechal Sobel, *The World They Made Together: Black and White Values in Eighteenth-Century Virginia* (Princeton, NJ: Princeton University Press, 1987), p. 48.
4. Ira Berlin, *Many Thousands Gone: The First Two Centuries of Slavery in North America* (Cambridge, MA: Harvard University Press, 1998), p. 30.
5. Finkelman, pp. 9, 89.
6. Ibid., pp. 5–6.

7. Ibid., p. 392.

8. Ibid., pp. 9, 89.

9. Thomas, p. 203.

10. Finkelman, p. 392.

11. Peter Kolchin, *American Slavery, 1619–1877* (New York, NY: Hill and Wang, 1993), p. 24.

12. Finkelman, p. 204.

13. Thomas, pp. 14–15.

14. Edmund S. Morgan, *American Slavery, American Freedom: The Ordeal of Colonial Virginia* (New York, NY: Norton, 1975), p. 328.

15. "Primary Reading Sources: Blacks and Virginia Law," *sitesALIVE!*, n.d., <http:// www.sitesalive.school.aol.com/tg/private/hlrwk4b. htm> (December 2, 2003).

16. Berlin, p. 119. www.sitesalive.school.aol.com/tg/private/hlrwk4b. htm (December 2, 2003).

17. Finkelman, p. 87.

18. Ibid., p. 392.

19. Ibid., p. 86.

CHAPTER 3. SLAVERY IN THE 18TH CENTURY

1. Ira Berlin, *Generations of Captivity* (Cambridge, MA: Harvard University Press, 2003), pp. 272–273.

2. Ibid.

3. Moses Grandy, "Narrative of the Life of Moses Grandy; Late a Slave in the United States of America: Electronic Edition," *University of North Carolina at Chapel Hill Libraries: Documenting the American South,* © 1996, <http://docsouth.unc.edu/grandy/ grandy.html> (December 2, 2003).

4. James Oakes, *Slavery and Freedom* (New York, NY: Knopf, 1990), p. 52.

5. Berlin, p. 274.

6. Ira Berlin, *Many Thousands Gone: The First Two Centuries of Slavery in North America* (Cambridge, MA: Harvard University Press, 1998), p. 146.

7. Paul Finkelman, ed., *Colonial Southern Slavery* (New York, NY: Garland Publishing, 1989), pp. 406, 408.

8. Lorena Walsh, *From Calabar to Carter's Grove: The History of a Virginia Slave Community* (Charlottesville, VA: University of Virginia Press, 1997), p. 83.

9. Mechal Sobel, *The World They Made Together: Black and White Values in Eighteenth- Century Virginia* (Princeton, NJ: Princeton University Press, 1987), p. 96.

10. Peter Kolchin, *American Slavery, 1619–1877* (New York, NY: Hill and Wang, 1993), p. 69.

11. Marvin L Michael Kay and Lorin Lee Cary, *Slavery in North Carolina, 1748–1775* (Chapel Hill, NC: University of North Carolina Press, 1995), p. 216.

12. Kolchin, p. 52.

13. Finkelman, p. 199.

14. Michele Gillespie, *Free Labor in an Unfree World: White Artisans in Slaveholding Georgia, 1789–1860* (Athens, GA: University of Georgia Press), p. 5; Finkelman, p. 205.

15. Sobel, p. 182.

16. Ibid., p. 144.

17. Hunter D. Farish, ed., *Journal and Letters of Philip Vickers Fithian, 1773–1774, A Plantation Tutor of the Old Dominion* (VA: Colonial Williamsburg, Inc., 1965), pp. 38–39.

18. Kolchin, p. 33.

19. Berlin, *Many Thousands Gone,* pp. 257–258.

20. Ibid., p. 263.

21. Ibid., p. 264.

22. John Hope Franklin and Alfred A. Moss, Jr., *From Slavery to Freedom: A History of African Americans* (New York, NY: McGraw-Hill, 1994), p. 85.

23. Berlin, *Many Thousands Gone,* p. 304.

CHAPTER 4. THE IMPACT OF COTTON ON SLAVERY

1. Charles Johnson and Patricia Smith, *Africans in America: America's Journey Through Slavery* (New York, NY: Harcourt Brace, 1998), pp. 267–268.

2. Peter Kolchin, *American Slavery, 1619–1877* (New York, NY: Hill and Wang, 1993), p. 95.

3. John Hope Franklin and Alfred Moss, *From Slavery to Freedom: A History of African Americans* (New York, NY: McGraw-Hill, 1994), p. 111; Kolchin, p. 96.

4. Kolchin, p. 101.

5. Johnson and Smith, p. 271.

6. Ibid., p. 272.

7. Franklin and Moss, p. 118.

8. Johnson and Smith, pp. 430, 433, 437.

9. James Oakes, *Slavery and Freedom* (New York, NY: Knopf, 1990), p. 140.

10. Henry Clay Bruce, "The New Man. Twenty-Nine Years a Slave. Twenty-Nine Years a Free Man," *University of North Carolina at Chapel Hill Libraries: Documenting the American South*, © 1997, http://docsouth.unc.edu/bruce/bruce.html (December 3, 2003).

11. Franklin and Moss, p. 129.

12. Ira Berlin, et al, eds., Remembering Slavery: *African Americans Talk About Their Personal Experiences of Slavery and Emancipation* (New York, NY: The New Press, 1998), p. 77.

13. Charles L. Perdue, Jr., Tomas E. Barden, and Robert K. Phillips, eds., *Weevils in the Wheat* (Charlottesville, VA: University Press of Virginia, 1976), p. 288.

14. Frederic Law Olmsted, *A Journey in the Seaboard Slave States* (New York, NY: New American Library, 1969), p. 91.

15. Ibid., p. 190.

16. Ibid., p. 241.

17. Oakes, p. 22.
18. Drew Gilpin Faust, *James Henry Hammond and the Old South* (Baton Rouge, LA: Louisiana State University Press, 1982), pp. 101–102.
19. Olmsted, pp. 386–387.
20. Berlin, *Remembering Slavery*, p. 89.
21. Franklin and Moss, p. 119.
22. Olmsted, p. 189.

CHAPTER 5. SLAVES AND MASTERS

1. James Henry Hammond, "James Henry Hammond advocates slavery," http://www.pbs.org/wgbh/aia/ part4/4h3439.html (March 18, 2004).
2. Drew Gilpin Faust, *James Henry Hammond and the Old South* (Baton Rouge, LA: Louisiana State University Press, 1982), p. 90
3. Charles L. Perdue, Jr., Tomas E. Barden, and Robert K. Phillips, eds., *Weevils in the Wheat* (Charlottesville, VA: University Press of Virginia, 1976), pp. 201–202.
4. Theodore Rosengarten, *Tombee: Portrait of a Cotton Planter* (New York, NY: William Morrow, 1986), p. 181.
5. Ibid.
6. Ibid., p. 488.
7. Louis Hughes, "Thirty Years a Slave. From Bondage to Freedom. The Institution of Slavery as Seen on the Plantation and in the Home of the Planter: Electronic Edition," *University of North Carolina at Chapel Hill Libraries: Documenting the American South,* © 1997, http://docsouth.unc.edu/hughes/hughes.html (December 3, 2003).
8. Paul Finkelman, ed., *Southern Slavery at the State and Local Level* (New York, NY: Garland, 1989), pp. 27–28.
9. Peter Kolchin, *American Slavery, 1619–1877* (New York, NY: Hill and Wang, 1993), p. 95.
10. Finkelman, p. 210.
11. Perdue, et. al., pp. 166–167.

12. Ibid., p. 183.

13. Ibid., pp. 182–183.

14. Ira Berlin, et al, eds., *Remembering Slavery: African Americans Talk About Their Personal Experiences of Slavery and Emancipation* (New York, NY: The New Press, 1998), p. 56.

15. Ariela Gross, *Double Character: Slavery and Mastery in the Antebellum Southern Courtroom* (Princeton, NJ: Princeton University Press, 2000), pp. 69–70.

16. Rosengarten, p. 122.

17. Ibid., p. 638.

18. James Oakes, *Slavery and Freedom* (New York, NY: Random House, 1990), p. 7.

19. Rosengarten, p. 157.

20. John Hope Franklin and Alfred Moss, *From Slavery to Freedom: A History of African Americans* (New York, NY: McGraw-Hill, 1994), p. 142.

21. Oakes, pp. 137–138.

22. Berlin, pp. 23–24.

23. Ibid., pp. 58–59.

24. John Blassingame, ed., *Slave Testimony: Two Centuries of Letters, Speeches, Interviews, and Autobiographies* (Baton Rouge, LA: Louisiana State University Press, 1989), p.49.

25. Berlin, pp. 64–70.

26. "Reflections, occasioned by the late Disturbances in Charleston," PBS, retrieved February 2015, http://www.pbs.org/wgbh/aia/part3/3h495.html.

CHAPTER 6. CULTURE AND SLAVE LIFE

1. Charles L. Perdue, Jr., Tomas E. Barden, and Robert K. Phillips, eds., *Weevils in the Wheat* (Charlottesville, VA: University Press of Virginia, 1976), p. 231.

2. Thomas Webber, *Deep Like the Rivers: Education in the Slave Quarter Community,* 1831–1865 (New York, NY: Norton, 1978), p. 214.

3. Ibid., p. 212.

4. Ira Berlin, et al, eds., *Remembering Slavery: African Americans Talk About Their Personal Experiences of Slavery and Emancipation* (New York, NY: The New Press, 1998), p.175.

5. Ibid., p. 171.

6. "Reflections, occasioned by the late Disturbances in Charleston," PBS, retrieved February 2015, http://www.pbs.org/wgbh/aia/part3/3h495.html.

7. Annie L. Burton, "Memories of Childhood's Slavery Days: Electronic Edition," *University of North Carolina at Chapel Hill Libraries: Documenting the American South,* ©1996, http://docsouth.unc.edu/burton/burton.html (December 3, 2003).

8. Perdue, et. al., p. 85.

9. Berlin, p. 140.

10. Peter Kolchin, *American Slavery, 1619–1877* (New York: Hill and Wang, 1993), p. 120.

11. John Hope Franklin and Alfred Moss, *From Slavery to Freedom: A History of African Americans* (New York: McGraw-Hill, 1994), p. 140.

12. Theodore Rosengarten, *Tombee: Portrait of a Cotton Planter* (New York: William Morrow, 1986), p. 347.

13. Junius Rodriguez, ed., *The Historical Encyclopedia of World Slavery* (Santa Barbara, CA.: ABC-CLIO, 1997), p. 220.

14. Charles Johnson and Patricia Smith, *Africans in America: America's Journey Through Slavery* (New York, NY: Harcourt Brace, 1998), p. 305.

15. Berlin, p. 145.

16. Dorothy Schneider and Carl Schneider, *American Experience: Slavery in America,* (New York, NY: Facts on File, 2007), p. 127.

17. "Urban Slavery" in "The Handbook of Texas Online," Texas State Historical Association, June 2010, https://tshaonline.org/handbook/online/articles/yps02.

18. Dorothy Schneider and Carl Schneider, *American Experience: Slavery in America* (New York, NY: Facts on File, 2007), p. 127.

19. "The Slaves Who Built Washington, D.C.," February 20, 2012, http://zmblackhistorymonth2012.blogspot.com/2012/02/slaves-who-built-washington-dc.

CHAPTER 7. EMANCIPATION

1. Theodore Rosengarten, *Tombee: Portrait of a Cotton Planter* (New York, NY: William Morrow, 1986), pp. 204–205.

2. Ira Berlin, et al, eds., *Remembering Slavery: African Americans Talk About Their Personal Experiences of Slavery and Emancipation* (New York, NY: The New Press, 1998), p. 259.

3. Ira Berlin and Leslie Rowland, *Families and Freedom: A Documentary History of African-American Kinship in the Civil War Era* (New York, NY: New Press, 1997), p. 78.

4. Ira Berlin, et al., eds., *Free At Last: A Documentary History of Slavery, Freedom, and the Civil War* (Edison, NJ: The Blue & Grey Press, 1997), pp. 3–6.

5. Ibid., p. 110.

6. Peter Kolchin, *American Slavery, 1619–1877* (New York, NY: Hill and Wang, 1993), p. 208.

7. Charles L. Perdue, Jr., Tomas E. Barden, and Robert K. Phillips, eds., *Weevils in the Wheat* (Charlottesville, VA: University Press of Virginia, 1976), p. 58.

8. Herbert George Gutman, *The Black Family in Slavery and Freedom* (New York, NY: Random House, 1977), p. 416.

9. Ibid., p. xxi.

10. Berlin and Rowland, pp. 214–215.

11. Nat Love, "The Life and Adventures of Nat Love Better Known in the Cattle Country as 'Deadwood Dick' by Himself; a True History of Slavery Days, Life on the Great Cattle Ranges and on the Plains of the 'Wild and Woolly' West, Based on Facts, and Personal

Experiences of the Author: Electronic Edition," *University of North Carolina at Chapel Hill Libraries: Documenting the American South*, © 1996, http://docsouth.unc.edu/neh/natlove/ natlove.html (December 3, 2003).

12. John Hope Franklin and Alfred Moss, *From Slavery to Freedom: A History of African Americans* (New York, NY: McGraw-Hill, 1994), p. 231.

13. Ibid., p. 234.

14. Berlin, p. 266.

GLOSSARY

amendment—An addition to a law or legal document that changes it forever.

emancipation—To free from bondage.

freedman—Former slave who is now free.

great house—The master's home.

indentured servants—Settlers who paid for their passage to America by working for a specified period of years.

master—A word for a person who owned slaves.

overseers—White employee of a slaveholder who was responsible for the work of slaves.

patterrollers—The name given to slave patrols by the slaves.

plantation—A large farm producing rice, tobacco, and sugar and other crops by slave labor.

ratify—Make something valid by giving official approval.

scrambling—Slaves purchased directly from slave ships by white plantation owners.

secede—To legally separate from a state or country to form a new and independent one.

servitude—Slavery or other condition in which one person worked for another.

sharecropping—Leasing land from an owner and paying for it with part of the proceeds of a crop.

slave codes—Laws passed by each slave state to control the lives of slaves.

slave driver—Supervisors who directed the work of the slaves.

slave patrols—Men hired by each Southern community to enforce the slave codes.

slave quarters—Cabins on a plantation where the slaves lived.

subservient—Under someone else.

task system—Method of working in which slaves were expected to finish a specific task each day.

triangular trade—A commercial route that took rum from Rhode Island to West Africa, where the rum was traded for slaves, who were brought to the West Indies, in return for sugar cane, used to make rum.

Underground Railroad—A collaboration of people who secretly worked to help slaves reach freedom in northern US states and Canada.

FURTHER READING

BOOKS

Bailey, Diane. *The Emancipation Proclamation and the End of Slavery in America*. New York, NY: The Rosen Publishing Group, 2015.

Baptiste, Tracey, ed. *The Civil War and Reconstruction Eras*. New York, NY: Britannica Educational Publishing in association with Rosen Educational Services, 2016.

Campbell, Ciara, ed. *Slavery in America*. New York, NY: Britannica Educational Publishing in association with Rosen Educational Services, 2016.

Diouf, Sylvaine. *Slavery's Exiles: The Stories of the Maroons*. New York, NY: New York University Press, 2013.

Fraser, Ian. *The Underground Railroad for Kids: The Amazing Stories and People of the Underground Railroad*. Kindle, 2015.

Hussey, Maria, ed. *The Rise of the Jim Crow Era*. New York, NY: Britannica Educational Publishing in association with Rosen Educational Services, 2016.

McGowan, James, and William Cashatus. *Harriet Tubman*. Santa Barbara, CA: Greenwood Press, 2011.

Nardo, Don. *Slavery Through The Ages*. San Diego, CA: Lucent Books, 2014.

Rasmusson, Daniel. *American Uprising: The Untold Story of America's Largest Slave Revolt*. New York, NY: Harper, 2011.

Sher, Abby. *Breaking Free: True Stories of Girls Who Escaped Slavery*. New York, NY: Barron's, 2014.

WEBSITES

American Slave Narratives

newdeal.feri.org/asn/asn00.htm

This archive contains narratives of several former slaves. These have been selected from an ambitious Works Progress Administration (WPA) project in the 1930s in which slaves were interviewed about their experiences.

Black History-History.Com

"Slavery in America."

www.history.com/topics/black-history/slavery

The history channel's article on slavery offers articles, videos, photographs, and speeches from the time when slavery was legal in America.

History.com

"Slavery in America Pictures & Galleries."

www.history.com/topics/black-history/slavery/photos

This photo gallery from History.com's site on Slavery in the United States features illustrations, photographs, broadsides, and political cartoons related to slavery.

INDEX

V

W